2 to 22 DAYS IN SPAIN AND PORTUGAL

THE ITINERARY PLANNER
1994 Edition

RICK STEVES

2 to 22 Days in Spain and Portugal Route

John Muir Publications
Santa Fe, New Mexico

Other JMP travel guidebooks by Rick Steves
Asia Through The Back Door (with Bob Effertz)
Europe Through the Back Door
Europe 101: History, Art, and Culture for the Traveler (with Gene Openshaw)
Kidding Around Seattle
Mona Winks: Self-Guided Tours of Europe's Top Museums (with Gene Openshaw)
2 to 22 Days in Europe
2 to 22 Days in France
2 to 22 Days in Great Britain
2 to 22 Days in Germany, Austria, and Switzerland
2 to 22 Days in Italy
2 to 22 Days in Norway, Sweden, and Denmark

Thanks to Dave Hoerlein, Mike McGregor, and Gene Openshaw for research assistance. Also to Gene Openshaw for editing. And to my wife, Anne, for her support and belief that someday I'll stay home.

John Muir Publications, P.O. Box 613, Santa Fe, NM 87504
© 1986, 1987, 1989, 1992, 1993, 1994 by Rick Steves
Cover and maps © 1986, 1987, 1989, 1992, 1993, 1994 by John Muir Publications
All rights reserved.
Printed in the United States of America
First printing, December 1993

ISSN 1058-6067
ISBN 1-56261-139-9

Cover Photo Leo de Wys Inc./Steve Vidler
Design Mary Shapiro
Maps Jim Wood and David C. Hoerlein
Typography Chris Brigman
Printer Banta Company

Distributed to the book trade by
W. W. Norton & Co., Inc.
New York, New York

Although the author and publisher have made every effort to provide accurate, up-to-date information, they accept no responsibility for loss, injury, or inconvenience sustained by any person using this book.

CONTENTS

HOW TO USE THIS BOOK

Like a grandpa bouncing a baby on his knee, Iberia is a mix of old and new, modern and traditional. Spain and Portugal can fill your travel days with traditional folk life, exotic foods, world-class art treasures, sunshine, friendly people, and palaces where the winds of the past can still be heard. And Iberia (especially Portugal) is still an inexpensive place to travel.

This book gives you the best 2 to 22 days in Spain and Portugal in a flexible plan. It sorts through all those "must see" sights, organizing the region into a carefully thought out, thoroughly tested, step-by-step itinerary. *2 to 22 Days in Spain and Portugal* is your problem-solver, your friendly fisherman, your helpful-in-a-jam Spaniard. It's your handbook for the best independent budget 2- to 22-day Iberian adventure.

Realistically, most travelers are interested in the predictable biggies—a bullfight, the Prado, and flamenco. This tour covers these biggies while mixing in a good dose of "back door" intimacy: sun-parched Andalusian hill towns, forgotten Algarve fishing villages, and desolate La Mancha windmills.

While the trip is designed as a car tour, it also makes a great three-week train/bus trip. Each day's journey is adapted for train and bus travel with explanations, options, and appropriate schedule information included.

The trip starts and ends in Madrid, but you might consider flying into Barcelona or Madrid and home from Lisbon (or vice versa). This "open jaws" flight plan saves lots of driving time and costs no more than flying in and out of the same city. Get specifics from your travel agent.

Flying from the U.S.A. to Madrid and back costs $600 to $1,000. For less than $500, you can split the cost of a car for three weeks or do this entire trip on first-class trains. For room and board, figure $50 a day for 22 days, totaling $1,100. This is a feasible budget, if you know the tricks. (If you don't, see my book, *Europe Through the Back Door.*) Students routinely eat and sleep through Spain and

Portugal for $30 a day. Add $400 fun money and you've got yourself a great Iberian holiday for around $2,800.

Read this book through completely before your trip. Use it as a rack to hang ideas on as your travel dream develops. As you study and travel and plan and talk to people, you'll fill it with notes. It's your tool.

The Layout

This book is flexible. It's completely modular and adaptable to an Iberian trip of any length. You'll find 22 "days," each built with the same sections:

1. **Introductory overview** of the day.
2. An hour-by-hour **Suggested Schedule** for each day.
3. **Transportation** plan for drivers, plus an adapted plan with schedules for train and bus travelers.
4. A **town orientation** with tourist information specifics, train information telephone number, and telephone area code.
5. List of the most important **Sightseeing Highlights** (rated: ▲▲▲ Don't miss; ▲▲ Try hard to see; ▲ Worthwhile if you can make it; no pyramids—a sight some find worth visiting).
6. **Food** and **Accommodations**: How and where to find the best budget places, including addresses, phone numbers, and my favorites.
7. An easy-to-read **map** locating recommended places.
8. **Itinerary Options** for those with more or less than the suggested time, or with particular interests.

At the back of the book, I've included thumbnail sketches of Spanish and Portuguese culture, history, art, and language, as well as lists of festivals, foreign phrases, a telephone directory, and other helpful information.

When to Go

Spring and fall offer the best combination of good weather, light crowds, long days, and plenty of tourist and cultural activities. Summer and winter travel each have their predictable pros and disappointing cons. July and August are most crowded in coastal areas, less crowded but uncomfortably hot and dusty in the interior. For weather specifics, see the climate chart in the Appendix. Whenever you anticipate crowds (like in July and August), call hotels in advance (call from one hotel to the next; your receptionist can help you) and try to arrive early.

Prices

A U.S. dollar is worth about 130 Spanish pesetas (ptas) and 160 Portuguese escudos. The Portuguese use a confusing dollar sign after the number of escudos (e.g., 120$00 or 120$).

For simplicity, I've listed hotels in the following price categories:

Hotel price category	US$	Spanish pesetas	Portuguese escudos
very cheap	under $17	under 2,200 ptas	under 2,700$
cheap	$17-26	2,300-3,300 ptas	2,700-4,000$
inexpensive	$26-45	3,300-5,500 ptas	4,000-7,000$
moderate	$45-65	5,500-8,000 ptas	7,000-10,000$
expensive	over $65	over 8,000 ptas	over 10,000$

The words "cheap," "inexpensive," "moderate," and "expensive" will be used when describing accommodations only to show these relative categories. These prices, as well as the hours and telephone numbers, are always changing, and I have tossed timidity out the window knowing you'll understand that this book, like any guidebook, starts growing old before it's even printed. Try to call ahead or double-check hours and times when you arrive. Expect about 10 percent inflation for many prices listed in this book.

My listings are for travelers with daily room-and-board budgets ranging from $25 to $70. The room rates I quote are for doubles (usually with private shower and breakfast). Singles generally cost one-third less than doubles. Triples and quads are plentiful and cheaper per person.

Telephoning
Using the telephone in your travels in Iberia is a bit more complicated but just as important as elsewhere in Europe. Always try to call ahead to confirm or reserve your room. With the new card-operated phones, it's a breeze—once you get the hang of the local area codes. See the telephone tips in the Appendix for help on phoning in Iberia

Tailoring the Book to Your Travel Pace
While this plan works (I get piles of "Having-a-great-trip" postcards from traveling readers), for some the pace is hectic. We Americans have about the shortest vacations in the rich world. We're notorious for traveling too fast. My goal is to offer maximum diversity and travel thrills with minimum redundancy at a fast but reasonable tempo. Skip things or add days according to your travel style and time constraints.

Your overall itinerary strategy is a fun challenge. Read through this book and note the problem days: Mondays, when many museums are closed, and Sundays, when public transportation is meager. Treat Saturdays as weekdays. It's good to mix intense and relaxed periods. Every trip needs at least a few slack days. Things like banking, laundry stops, mail, and picnics should be anticipated and planned for.

Train travelers should realize that the trains in Spain are sometimes a pain, making the full 22-day itinerary impractical. Train travelers will want to streamline with overnight train rides and skip a few out-of-the-way places, as recommended in the text.

Thinking Ahead
Ad-libbing a holiday through Spain and Portugal sounds fine, but those with limited time and money can't afford the serious mistakes that plague careless travelers. An itinerary enables you to hit the festivals, bullfights, and museums on the right day. Travelers who plan ahead experience more, save time, and spend less money. Those who routinely use the telephone do even better. Study the phone tips in the Appendix.

This itinerary assumes you are a well-organized traveler who lays departure groundwork upon arrival. Keep a list of all the things that should be taken care of, and ward off problems whenever possible before they happen. Use local tourist information centers; don't be an "Ugly American." If you expect to travel smart, you will. If you insist on being confused, your trip will be a mess.

General Warning: Tourists are prime targets for thieves throughout Spain and Portugal, especially in Barcelona, Seville and Lisbon. While hotel rooms are generally safe and muggings are very rare, cars are commonly broken into, purses are snatched, and pockets are picked. Be on guard, wear a money belt, assume any commotion around you is there as a theft smoke screen, leave nothing of value in your car, and park carefully. When traveling by train, keep your rucksack in sight and—particularly on overnight trains—clip it to the luggage rack for safety.

Recommended Guidebooks

This small book is your itinerary handbook. To thoroughly enjoy and appreciate these three busy weeks, you may want supplemental information. Sure, it hurts to spend $30 or $40 on extra guidebooks, but when you consider the improvements they will make in your $3,000 vacation—not to mention the money they'll save you—they can be a good investment. Here is my recommended guidebook strategy.

General low-budget directory-type guidebooks—The best I've found are *Let's Go: Spain, Portugal and Morocco* and the *Rough Guides* to Spain and Portugal. *Let's Go,* updated each year by Harvard students, has ten times the information on these countries and one-tenth the readership of the great *Let's Go: Europe* guidebook. Its approach is cool, youthful, and train-oriented. I've assumed that anyone interested in the night scene will have *Let's Go.* If you've got $60 a day for room and board, you may be a little rich for some of its recommendations, but, especially if you're going to Morocco, it's the best information source around ($14.95, 610 pages, new editions come out each December). The *Rough Guides* to

Spain and Portugal are written for young vagabonds traveling on a shoestring and therefore weak in hotel listings, their wealth of background material and cultural insights make them worthwhile for those traveling on any budget.

Older travelers like the style of Arthur Frommer's Spain/Morocco and Portugal guides even though they, like the Fodor guides, ignore alternatives that enable travelers to save money by dirtying their fingers in the local culture.

Cultural and sightseeing guides—*Michelin's Green Guides* for Spain and Portugal are great for information on sights and culture, though they contain nothing on room and board. They are written with the driver in mind (on Michelin tires, of course). James Michener's *Iberia* is great pretrip reading for background on the area's culture. The well-written and thoughtful Cadogan guides to Spain and Portugal are excellent for A students on the road. The encyclopedic *Blue Guides* to Spain and Portugal are dry and scholastic but just right for some people.

Maps—Michelin makes the best. They're available and inexpensive throughout Iberia. Firestone maps in Spain are also good.

Rick Steves's books—I've written this book assuming (or at least hoping) you have read the latest edition of my book on the skills of budget travel, *Europe Through the Back Door*. To keep this book small and pocket-sized, I've resisted the temptation to repeat the most applicable and important information already included in *Europe Through the Back Door*; there is no overlap. *Europe Through the Back Door* gives you the basic skills of traveling on your own, the foundation that makes this demanding 2- to 22-day plan possible. There are chapters on minimizing jet lag, packing light, driving or train travel, finding budget beds without reservations, changing money, theft and the tourist, hurdling the language barrier, health, travel photography, long-distance telephoning in Europe, travelers' toilet trauma, ugly-Americanism, itinerary strategies, and how to wash your entire wardrobe in a sink with no plug.

Europe 101: History and Art for the Traveler (with Gene Openshaw) gives you the story of Europe's people, history, and art, preparing you to understand the sights of Iberia, from Roman times through the Inquisition and up to the Spanish Civil War. *Mona Winks: Self-Guided Tours of Europe's Top Museums* (also with Gene Openshaw) has a chapter outlining the best three-hour visit to Madrid's overwhelming Prado Museum.

Europe Through the Back Door Spanish/Pourtugese Phrase Book—Spain and Portugal each come with a serious language barrier. This phrasebook is designed to help you communicate your way through a smooth and inexpensive trip. It gives you all the key phrases as well as a traveler's dictionary. Your bookstore should have these four books (all published by John Muir Publications, Santa Fe, NM).

Apart from books, a traveler's best friends are the tourist offices (Turismos) you'll find throughout Spain and Portugal. Use them for things like maps, accommodations, where to find a pharmacy, driving instructions, and recommendations for night life. Most Turismos have information on the entire country. When you visit a Turismo (abbreviated TI in this book), remember to pick up maps for towns you'll be visiting later on your trip.

Accommodations

Spain and Portugal offer some of the the cheapest rooms in Europe. Most accommodations are government-regulated with posted prices. While Easter, July, and August are often crowded, I've never needed reservations. Even so, to get exactly the place I want, I often call in the morning to secure a room for that day's destination.

While prices are low, street noise is often high (Spaniards are notorious night owls). Always ask to see your room first. You can check the price posted on the door, consider potential night noise problems, ask for another room, or bargain the price down. Breakfast and showers can cost extra, and meals may or may not be required—always ask. In many cases, hotels charge extra for showers "down the hall." In most towns, the best places to look for rooms are in the old (and most interesting) quarter, near the main church, Plaza Mayor, and most sights.

Don't judge places by their bleak and dirty entryways. Landlords often stand firmly in the way of hardworking hoteliers who'd like to brighten their buildings up. Off-season prices are soft.

Both Spain and Portugal have plenty of youth hostels and campgrounds, but I don't recommend them. Youth hostels are often a headache, campgrounds are hot and dusty, and the savings, considering the great bargains on other accommodations, are not worth the trouble. Hotels and pensions are easy to find, inexpensive, and, when chosen properly, an important part of experiencing the Spanish and Portuguese cultures. If you're on a starvation budget or just want to camp or hostel, there is plenty of information available through the National Tourist Office and in appropriate guidebooks.

Each country has its handy categories of accommodations. In Spain, government-regulated places have blue and white plaques outside their doors clearly marked F, CH, P, HsR, HR, Hs, or H. Despite the different names, all are basically "hotels" offering different services. These are, in ascending order of price and comfort: Fonda (F) is your basic simple inn, often with a small bar serving cheap meals. A Casa de Huéspedes (CH) is a guest house without a bar. Pensiones (P) are like CHs but serve meals. Hostales (Hs) have nothing to do with youth hostels. They are quite comfortable, are rated from one to three stars, and charge \$30 to \$60 for a double. Hotels (H) are rated with one to five stars and go right up to world-class luxury places. Hostal-Residencias (HsR) and Hotel-Residencias (HR) are the same as Hs and H class with no meals except breakfast.

Any regulated place will have a *libro de reclamaciones* (complaint book). A request for this book will generally solve any problem you have in a jiffy.

Portugal's system starts at the bottom with Residencias, Albergarias, and Pensões (one to four stars). These pensions are Portugal's best accommodation value—cheap (\$30-\$40 doubles) and often tasteful, traditional, comfy, and family run. Hotels (one to five stars) are more expensive (\$30-\$100 doubles).

Both Spain and Portugal have local bed-and-breakfast accommodations, usually in touristy areas where locals decide to open up a spare room and make a little money on the side. Ask for a *cama, habitacion*, or *casa particulare* in Spain and a *quarto* or *casa particulare* in Portugal. They are very cheap ($10 to $15 per bed), always interesting, and usually a good experience.

Spain and Portugal also have luxurious government-sponsored historic inns. These *paradores* (Spain) and *pousadas* (Portugal) are often renovated castles, palaces, or monasteries, many with great views and stately atmosphere. While they can be a good value (doubles from $70-$150, reservations often necessary), I find many of them sterile, stuffy, and overly impressed with themselves, much like the tourists who stay there. I enjoy wandering through them and having an occasional breakfast with real silver and too much service. But for the best sleeping value, you can find what I call "poor man's paradores"—elegant normal places that offer double the warmth and Old World intimacy for half the price.

Eating in Spain

Spaniards eat to live, not vice versa. Their cuisine is hearty food of the people in big, inexpensive portions.

While not fancy, there is an endless variety of regional specialties. The two most famous Spanish dishes are *paella* and *gazpacho*. Paella has a base of saffron-flavored rice as background for whatever the chef wants to mix in—seafood, chicken, peppers, and so forth. Gazpacho, an Andalusian specialty, is a chilled soup of tomatoes, bread chunks, and spices that really hits the spot on a hot day. Garlic and olive oil are very common in Spanish cooking.

The Spanish eating schedule frustrates many visitors. Because most Spaniards work until 19:30, supper (*cena*) is usually served around 21:00 or 22:00, or even later. Lunch (*comida*) is also served late (13:00-16:00) and is the largest meal of the day. Don't buck this system. No good restaurant will serve meals at American hours.

The only alternative to this late schedule, and my choice for a quick dinner, is to eat in tapa bars. Tapas are small portions, like appetizers, of all kinds of foods—seafood, salads, meat-filled pastries, deep-fried tasties, and on and on—normally displayed under glass at the bar (about $1). *Raciónes* are larger portions of tapas—more like a full meal (about $3). Common tapas items include *chorizo* (spicy sausage), *gambas* (shrimp), *calamares fritos* (fried squid rings), *jamon serrano* (cured ham), *queso* (cheese), and *tortilla española* (potato omelette). *Bocadillos* (sandwiches) are cheap and basic. A ham sandwich is just that—ham on bread, period.

Other budget eating options are *platos combinados* (combination plates) which usually include portions of one or two main dishes, a vegetable, and bread for a reasonable price; or the *menu del dia* (menu of the day), a substantial three-to-four course meal that often includes a beverage. A common dessert is *flan* (caramel custard). *Helado* (ice cream) is popular, as is *blanco y negro*, a vanilla-ice-cream-and-coffee float.

The price of a tapa, beer, or coffee is cheapest if you eat or drink standing at the bar or sitting on a bar stool. You may pay a little more to eat sitting at a table and still more for an outdoor table. In the right place, a quiet coffee break on the town square is well worth the extra charge. But the cheapest seats sometimes get the best show. Sit at the bar and study your bartender—he's an artist. For a quick and substantial breakfast, order *tortilla española* (potato omelet) with your *café solo* (black) or *café con leche* (white) in any café.

When searching for a good bar, I look for the noisy places with ankle-deep piles of napkins and food debris on the floor, lots of locals, and the TV blaring. "Cheers" is on almost nightly, and it's fun to watch in Spanish. Other popular TV shows include bullfights and soccer games, as well as Spanish versions of silly game shows and soaps.

Spain produces some excellent wine, both red (*tinto*) and white (*blanco*). Major wine regions include Valdepenas, Penedes and Rioja. Sherry is a fortified wine from the Jerez region. *Sangria* (red wine mixed with fruit juice) is popular and refreshing. Spain has good, cheap, boxed orange juice. Portugal doesn't, but serves delicious fresh-

Public Transportation

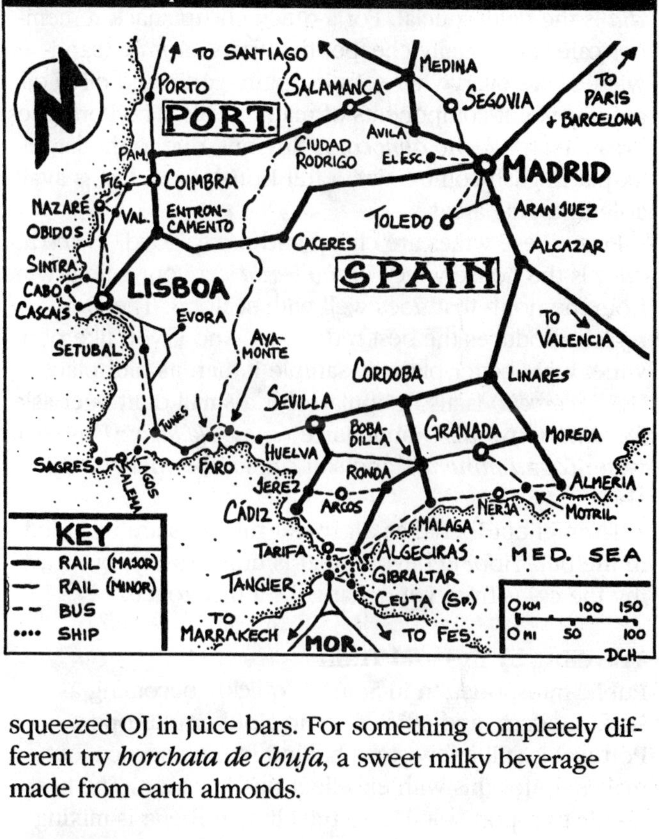

squeezed OJ in juice bars. For something completely different try *horchata de chufa*, a sweet milky beverage made from earth almonds.

Eating in Portugal

The Portuguese meal schedule is a bit less cruel, though still late. Lunch (*almoco*) is the big meal, served between noon and 14:00, while supper (*jantar*) is from 20:00 to 22:00. Perhaps as a result, tapas are not such a big deal. You can eat—and eat well—in restaurants for $6.

Seafood lovers will be in heaven—along the coast, chances are you were swimming yesterday with what's on your plate today. Fish soup *(sopa de peixe)* or shellfish soup (*sopa de mariscos*) are worth seeking out. *Caldo verde* is a popular vegetable soup. *Frango assado* is roast chicken; ask for *piri-piri* sauce if you like it hot and spicy. *Porco a alentejana* is an interesting combination of pork and clams. *Meia dose* means half portion, while *prato do dia* is the daily special. For a quick cheap snack remember cafés are usually cheaper than bars. *Sandes* (sandwiches) are everywhere. As in Spain, garlic and olive oil are important components of many meals. The Portuguese breakfast (*pequeno almoco*) is tiny but, due to the large ex-pat English community, a full British breakfast is available in tourist areas.

Portuguese wines are cheap and pretty good. *Vinho da casa* is the house wine. *Vinho verde* is a young light wine from the north that goes well with seafood. The *Dao* region produces the best red wines. And if you like port wine, what better place to sample it than its birthplace. Beer (*cerveja*) is also popular—for a small draft beer ask for *uma imperial.* Orange juice *(sumo de laraja),* mineral water *(agua mineral),* and soft drinks are widely available.

Throughout Iberia, as a general rule, tips are included in the bill. Tipping beyond that is unnecessary, but leaving the coins from your change is a nice touch.

Traveling by Bus and Train

Public transportation in Spain is quickly becoming as slick, modern, and efficient as in Northern Europe. Portugal is still a few steps behind in train service, but makes up for this with excellent bus transport. The best public transport solution to traveling in Iberia is mixing bus and train travel, taking advantage of the best services of each mode. This 22-day itinerary would require about 7-8 bus days and 4-5 train days to do efficiently. Always verify bus or train schedules before arriving at the station. I never leave a bus or train station without my next day's schedule options in hand.

Railpasses

Both Spain and Portugal offer railpasses that allow travel for a given number of days for a fixed period of time (4 days in a 15-day period in Portugal for about $95, first class only, and 3 days out of a month period in Spain for about $180 first class, about $140 second class). While you could save money by purchasing point-to-point tickets as you go, you may find the convenience of the railpasses worth the extra cost. Spain and Portugal also offer a combination short-term car rental and railpass deal that you should consider seriously if you want to explore some of the more off-the-beaten-path places in this book. (In Spain, 3 days of car and 3 days of second class train travel in a month period is about $205 per person, assuming two persons traveling together; the same package costs about $135 per person in Portugal.) A three-week Eurailpass costs $648 (first class) and pays for itself on this tour only if you're traveling to Spain from the north (Paris to Madrid costs $135 second class). Remember, this tour uses lots of buses, where Eurail is worthless.

It costs about $50 for the long second-class train rides from Madrid to Barcelona, Lisbon, Sevilla, and Granada. First class is 50 percent more. Most overnight trains have $12 sleeping berths (*coche-litera*). A *coche-cama*, or private berth, in a classy double compartment costs only a couple of dollars more. I go overnight whenever possible in Spain. Even with a train pass, reservations are required on any long (over 3 hours) Spanish train rides. Reserve your seat on the departing train as soon as you arrive in a town, either at the station or at a RENFE office in the town center. Note: train business is easiest to take care of in the downtown RENFE offices.

RENFE (the acronym for the Spanish national train system) categorizes its trains as very slow mail trains (*correo*), pretty slow but faster than a burro (*tranvias* and *semi-directos*), fast (*expreso* and *rapido*), and super luxury (*ter*, *electro*, and *talgo*). The new high-speed train called the AVE (requiring a supplement) whisks travelers between Madrid and Seville in under 3 hours. Trains get more expensive as they pick up speed, but all are much cheaper per mile than their northern European counterparts.

Portugal doesn't have the same categories as Spain. It has mostly slow, milk-run trains and an occasional Expreso. Off the main Lisbon-Porto-Coimbra lines, buses are a better bet.

Since Iberian trains are often late, phone the station to confirm departure times (telephone numbers are listed throughout this book). Remember, you may arrive at the station an hour after a train has left—according to the schedule—and still catch it. But plan on being early if you need to buy a ticket, since that can be a time-consuming headache.

For the complete schedule and explanation of the Spanish train system, pick up the *Guía RENFE* (cheap at any station). In Spain, *Salidas* means departures, *Llegadas* is arrivals; in Portugal, *Partidas* and *Chegadas* are departures and arrivals, respectively.

Bus Transport in Spain and Portugal

Buses will take you where trains don't. In cases where bus and trains serve the same destination, the bus is often more efficient. Read the daily itinerary in this book before selecting the best mode of travel for that day. Don't leave a bus station to explore a city without knowing your next schedule options and making reservations if necessary. Always reserve longer-distance buses ahead. Sunday bus service can be dismal, so plan ahead and verify schedules. In the countryside, stop buses by waving. There are no buspass options, so all tickets must be purchased at the station or in travel agencies that sell bus tickets. Ask at the tourist office for travel agencies selling bus tickets (they can also reserve a seat) to save you time if the bus station is not central.

Traveling by Car

Driving in Iberia is great, although major roads can be clogged by endless caravans of slow-moving trucks. Car rental is as cheap as anywhere in Europe—about $150 a week with unlimited mileage, through your hometown travel agent. I'd pay extra for the Collision Damage Waiver (CDW) supplement. Iberia is rough on cars and you don't need the mental overhead of the giant deductibles. While the International Drivers License is officially required (available cheap and easy from AAA, bring two old photos), many manage with only their state drivers licenses.

You'll need a credit card for security. The Spanish version of AAA is the Real Automobil Club; in Portugal it's the Automovil Clube de Portugal.

Drive very defensively. If you have an accident, you will be blamed and in for a monumental headache. Seat belts are required by law. Gas and diesel prices are controlled and the same everywhere (around $3.50 a gallon for gas, less for diesel). *Gasolina* is either "normal" or "super" (unleaded is now widely available), and diesel is called *gasoleo.* Expect to be stopped for a routine check by the police (be sure your car insurance form is up to date). There are plenty of speed traps. Tickets are issued and paid for on the spot. Portugal is statistically one of Europe's most dangerous places to drive. You'll notice a lot of ambulances on the road.

Have a copy of your key made right away for safety and convenience. Choose parking places carefully. Leave valuables in the trunk during the day and leave **nothing** worth stealing in the car overnight. While you should avoid parking lots with twinkly asphalt, thieves break car windows anywhere, even at stop lights. The police recommend leaving your car unlocked at night, the glove compartment open, and if it's a hatchback, taking the trunk cover off so thieves can look in without breaking in. Parking attendants all over Spain holler, "*Nada en el coche*"—nothing in the car. And they mean it. Ask at your hotel for advice on parking. In cities you can park safely but expensively in guarded lots.

Raise Your Travel Dreams to Their Upright and Locked Position

This book is designed to free you, not chain you. Defend your spontaneity as you would your mother. Use this book to avoid time- and money-wasting mistakes, to get more intimate with Iberia by traveling as a temporary local person, and as a point of departure from which to shape your best possible travel experience.

Anyone who has read this far has what it takes intellectually to do this tour on their own. With the information in this book and a determination to travel smart, you can expect a smooth trip. Be confident and militantly positive; relish the challenge and rewards of doing your own planning. Judging from all the positive feedback and happy postcards we receive from those who traveled with earlier editions of this book, it's safe to assume you're on your way to a great Iberian vacation—independent, inexpensive, and with the finesse of an experienced traveler.

Send Me a Postcard, Drop Me a Line

While I do what I can to keep this book accurate and up-to-date, you can't step in the same Iberian river twice. If you enjoy a successful trip with the help of this book and would like to share your discoveries (and help me out), please send any tips, recommendations, criticisms, or corrections to me at Europe Through the Back Door, 109 4th N., Box 2009, Edmonds, WA 98020. All correspondents will receive a two-year subscription to our "Back Door Travel" quarterly newsletter (it's free anyway), and recommendations used will get you a first-class railpass in heaven. Thanks, and happy travels!

BACK DOOR PHILOSOPHY

AS TAUGHT IN *EUROPE THROUGH THE BACK DOOR*

Travel is intensified living—maximum thrills per minute and one of the last great legal sources of adventure. In many ways, the less you spend, the more you get.

Experiencing the real thing requires candid informality—going "Through the Back Door."

Affording travel is a matter of priorities. Many people who "can't afford a trip" could sell their cars and travel for two years.

You can travel anywhere in the world for $50 a day plus transportation costs. Money has little to do with enjoying your trip. In fact, spending more money builds a thicker wall between you and what you came to see.

A tight budget forces you to travel "close to the ground," meeting and communicating with the people, not relying on service with a purchased smile. Never sacrifice sleep, nutrition, safety, or cleanliness in the name of budget. Simply enjoy the local-style alternatives to expensive hotels and restaurants.

Extroverts have more fun. If your trip is low on magic moments, kick yourself and start making things happen.

If you don't enjoy a place, it's often because you don't know enough about it. Seek the truth. Recognize tourist traps.

A culture is legitimized by its existence. Give a people the benefit of your open mind. Think of things as different but not better or worse.

Of course, travel, like the world, is a series of hills and valleys. Be fanatically positive and militantly optimistic.

Travel is addicting. It can make you a happier American as well as a citizen of the world. Our Earth is home to more than five billion equally important people. It's wonderfully humbling to travel and find that people don't envy Americans. They like us, but with all due respect, they wouldn't trade passports.

Globe-trotting destroys ethnocentricity and encourages the understanding and appreciation of various cultures. Travel changes people. Many travelers toss aside their "hometown blinders," assimilating the best points of different cultures into their own character.

The world is a cultural garden. We're tossing the ultimate salad. Raise your travel dreams to their upright and locked position and join us.

ITINERARY

DAYS 1 and 2 Settle down in Madrid, shift into Spanish gear (late meals, siestas), *habla un poco Español*, and see the major sights of Spain's major city. With Europe's best collection of paintings, its third-best royal palace, a mega-flea market, and enough street-singing, bar-hopping, people-watching vitality to give any visitor a boost of youth, Madrid is the place to start your three-week Iberian adventure.

DAY 3 Spain's history is lavish, brutal, and complicated. Tour the imposing El Escorial palace, sternly elegant and steeped in history. Then pay tribute to the countless victims of Spain's Civil War at the awesome Valley of the Fallen. Set up in Segovia and enjoy its Roman aqueduct and a succulent roast pig.

DAY 4 Spend the morning in Segovia's romantic castle and musty cathedral before traveling to Salamanca, a living textbook of history and architecture, where you'll find the ultimate Spanish town square and Spain's most historic university, swaddled in a strolling college-town ambience.

DAY 5 Next it's on to Portugal, stopping for a climb through the medieval turrets and mossy crannies of little Ciudad Rodrigo on the way to the university town of Coimbra, the most user-friendly city in Portugal. Explore the university, old cathedral, and old quarter of what was Portugal's leading city.

DAY 6 After a few extra hours in Portugal's "Oxford," drop by the patriotic pride and architectural joy of Portugal, the Batalha monastery. If the spirit moves you, the pilgrimage sight at Fatima is just down the road. Find a hotel at nearby Nazaré, an Atlantic coast fishing town that reeks with tradition while comfortably accommodating its visitors. Fill yourself with shrimp.

DAY 7 After all the traveling you've done, it's high time for an easy day and some fun in the Portuguese sun. Your beach town, surrounded by cork groves, eucalyptus trees, ladies who wear seven petticoats, and men who stow cigarettes and fish hooks in their stocking caps, offers the perfect mix of sun, sand, and seafood, with enough salty fishing village atmosphere to make you pucker.

DAYS 8 and 9 After a stop at the almost edibly cute walled town of Ójbidos, plunge into Portugal's capital and largest city, Lisbon. The closest thing to an urban jungle on this trip, Lisbon is a yellowed scrapbook of trolleys, sailors' quarters, mournful folk music, and Old-World elegance caked in twentieth-century squalor. There's plenty to see, do, eat, and drink.

DAY 10 Take a side trip from Lisbon directly into Portugal's seafaring glory days. After a morning of royal coaches, elegant cloisters, and maritime memories in the suburb of Belem, you'll head for the hills to climb through the Versailles of Portugal, the Pena Palace. Then, following a romp along the ruined ramparts of a deserted Moorish castle on a neighboring hilltop and a short walk out to Portugal's wind-lashed westernmost point, you'll finish the day dining, gambling, or strolling along the beachfront promenade of a past-its-prime resort town, Cascais or Estoril.

DAYS 11 and 12 After big-city Lisbon, you'll enjoy a day and a half in a sleepy fishing village on the south coast and a chance for some rigorous rest and intensive relaxation on Portugal's best beach. Your Algarve hideaway is sunny Salema. It's just you, a handful of fishermen, your wrinkled landlady, and a few other globe-trotting experts-in-lethargy. Nearby sightseeing possibilities include Cape Sagres, Europe's "Land's End" and home of Henry the Navigator's famous navigation school, and the jet-setty resort of Lagos. Or you could just work on a tan and see how slow you can get your pulse in sleepy Salema.

DAYS 13 and 14 If your solar cells are recharged, roll up your beach towel and meander across the Algarve into Spain for your Sevilla experience. The city of Carmen, flamenco, Don Giovanni, and the 1992 World's Fair has its share of impressive sights, but the real magic is in its ambience: its quietly tangled Jewish Quarter, riveting flamenco shows, thriving bars, and teeming paseo. Spend your evening in the streets, rafting through a choppy river of Spanish humanity.

DAYS 15 and 16 Leave Sevilla early to wind through the golden hills of the "Ruta de Pueblos Blancos" in search of Andalusia's most exotic whitewashed villages. After a night in the region's romantic capital, Arcos de la Frontera, and a leisurely morning, drop by Jerez for a peek at its famous horses in action and a sherry bodega tour (with smooth samples). Then, it's on to the least-touristed piece of Spain's generally overtouristed south coast: the whitewashed, almost Arabic-flavored port of Tarifa.

DAY 17 Ooo Morocco! For something entirely different, take the hydrofoil day trip from Tarifa to Tangiers. Admittedly, Tangiers is the Tijuana of Morocco, but the excellent one-day tour from Tarifa will fill your day with a whirlpool of carpets, tea, belly dancers, donkey dust, camel snorts, and medina memories. This kind of cultural voyeurism is almost like visiting the devil, but it's non-stop action and as memorable as an audit.

DAY 18 After your day in Africa, a day in England may sound jolly good. And that's just where you're going today—to the land of tea and scones, fish and chips, pubs and bobbies—Gibraltar. After this splash of uncharacteristically sunny England, enter the bikini-strangled land of basted bodies on the beach, the Costa del Sol. Bed down in this congested region's closest thing to pleasant, the happy town of Nerja, for a firsthand look at Europe's beachy playground.

DAYS 19 and 20 Enjoy a beach-easy morning on the Costa del Sol and a crawl through the stalagmighty Nerja caves, then say "Adiós" to the Mediterranean and head into the rugged Sierra Nevada mountains to the historic city of Granada. Famous as the last stronghold of the Moorish kingdom, Granada has the incomparable Alhambra palace and an exotically tangled Arab Quarter. After a day and a half here, you'll know why they say, "There's nothing crueler than being blind in Granada."

DAYS 21 and 22 The 250-mile trip north through the windmills and castles of La Mancha and dusty memories of Don Quixote takes you to Toledo, the historic, artistic, and spiritual capital of Spain. Incredibly well preserved and full of cultural wonder, the entire city has been declared a national historical monument. Toledo teems with tourists, souvenirs, and great art by day, delicious roast suckling pig, echoes of El Greco, and medieval magic by night. It's a great finale for your 22 days in Spain and Portugal. You're just an hour south of your trip's starting point—Madrid. Adiós!

DAY 1 AND 2

MADRID

Depart the U.S.A.

Call to confirm your scheduled departure time before going to the airport. Expect delays. Bring something—a book, a journal, some handwork, an infant—to keep yourself occupied. Remember: no matter how long it takes, flying to Europe is a luxury. If you arrive safely on the day you hoped to, the flight is a smashing success.

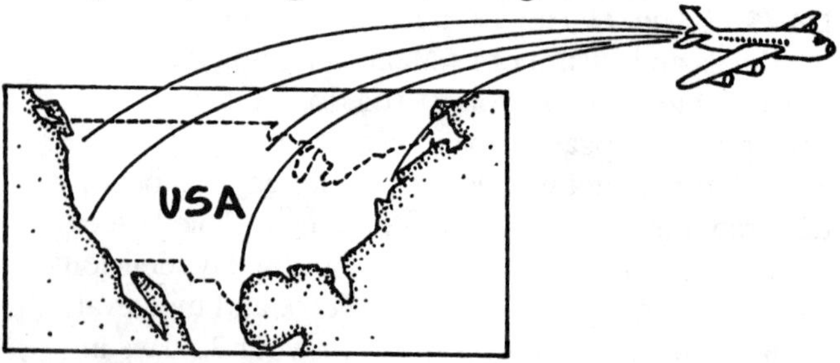

To minimize jet lag

■ Leave healthy and well rested. Pretend you're leaving a day earlier than you really are. Plan accordingly and enjoy a peaceful last day.

■ During the flight, minimize stress to your system by eating lightly and avoiding alcohol, caffeine, and sugar. A flight dehydrates you. Say, "Two orange juices, no ice, please," every chance you get. Take walks.

■ After boarding the plane, set your watch ahead to European time; start adjusting mentally before you land.

■ Sleep through the in-flight movie—or at least close your eyes and fake it.

■ On the day you arrive, keep yourself awake until a reasonable local bedtime. Jet lag hates fresh air, bright light, and exercise. A long evening city walk is helpful.

■ You'll probably wake up very early the next morning—but ready to roll.

Arrive in Madrid

You fast-forward a day flying to Europe: if you leave on a Tuesday, you'll land on Wednesday. Spend Day One getting acquainted with Madrid.

On this first day in Madrid, you'll be set up by evening. If you just flew in, jet lag will lower its sleepy boom too early. An evening walk is a cool, enjoyable, breathe-deep way to stay awake until a reasonable bedtime on your first night in Europe.

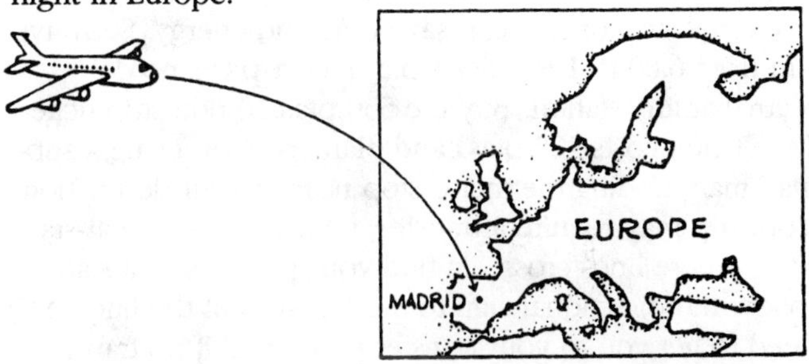

By plane: Madrid's Barajas Airport is ten miles east of downtown. It has a 24-hour bank with fair rates. You'll also find a tourist desk (8:00-20:00, Saturday 9:00-13:00, closed Sunday, tel. 305-8656, with English-speaking and helpful personnel, a free Madrid map, a subway map, and a good supply of maps and town information brochures for all of Spain—see list of what to get under Madrid orientation, below), a telephone office where you can buy a phone card, a RENFE desk for rail information, a pharmacy, on-the-spot car rental agencies, and easy public transportation into town. Use your phone card and call to confirm your hotel, then take the yellow bus into Madrid—it leaves four times an hour for Plaza Colón (300 ptas, 30-minute ride—airport taxis are far more expensive, though not outrageous). From Plaza Colón take the subway to your hotel (see subway information below). To find the nearest subway stop, walk past the modern sculpture on Plaza Colon and cross the street.

By train: If you're arriving by train from France or Barcelona, you'll land at the modern Chamartin station. While you're at the station, pick up sightseeing information at the helpful tourist office (see list of what to get under Madrid orientation), change money if you need to, and make a reservation for your departure. Remember, in Spain, train rides longer than about 3 hours require reservations, even with a Eurailpass. Ride the subway into town.

Transportation in Madrid

Madrid's subway—cheap (especially the ten rides for 550 ptas strip ticket) and simple—is understandably the pride of the Spanish public transportation system. The city's broad streets can be hot and exhausting. A subway trip of even a stop or two can save time and energy. Subways run from 6:00 to 1:30. Pick up a free map (Plano del Metro) at any station. Buy the 550 ptas 10 ride strip ticket (one ticket costs 125 ptas) and plan your trip using a subway map, finding the metro stop nearest your destination. Your trip may require a transfer, which is possible at stations where lines cross. To find your platform in a station, follow the directional sign to the last stop of the line you need to get you to your transfer point, and if no transfer is needed, to your final stop. Insert your ticket in the turnstile and retrieve it as you pass through. *Salida* means exit and the signs are green.

City buses, not so cheap or easy, can be helpful. Get details and schedules at the booth on Puerta del Sol. Taxis are expensive: figure 1600 ptas from the Chamartin station to Puerta del Sol.

Avoid driving in Madrid. Rent your car when you're ready to leave. Ideally, you should make car rental arrangements through your travel agent before you leave home. In Madrid, try Europcar (San Leonardo 8, tel. 541-8892, airport: 305-4420), Hertz (Jacomatrezzo 15, tel. 541-7086, airport: 305-8452), or Avis (Gran Vía 60, tel. 547-2048, airport: 305-8532). Call to see if your car can be delivered free to your hotel.

Transportation from Madrid

The two main rail stations, Atocha and Chamartin, are both on subway lines and easily accessible from anywhere in the city. Some confusion is caused by the fact that there are two Atocha stations. The metro stop Atocha RENFE is not the main train station. Each has all the services a traveler needs: banks, car rental, and information desks. Train information: 429-0202 or 522-0518.

The two key bus stations are both on metro lines as well: Estacion La Sepulvedana at Po. de la Florida, metro

Norte (service to Segovia); and Estacion Herranz, on C. Fernandez de los Rios metro Moncloa (service to El Escorial).

Sightseeing in Madrid

Dive headlong into the historic grandeur and intimate charms of Spain's capital. The lavish Royal Palace, with its gilded rooms and frescoed ceilings, rivals Versailles. Madrid's huge Retiro Park invites you for a shady siesta and a hopscotch through a mosaic of lovers, families, skateboarders, pets walking their masters, and old-time bench-sitters. Make time for Madrid's elegant shops, people-friendly pedestrian zones, and, if it's Sunday, for the flea market and a bullfight. The canvas highlights of the great Prado Museum, and Picasso's stirring *Guernica*, are a must.

Suggested Schedule Day 1

8:00	Brisk, good morning Madrid walk, 20 minutes from Sol to Prado, stopping for breakfast.
9:00	Prado Museum, tour Europe's best collection of paintings.
12:00	See Picasso's *Guernica* at the Reina Sofia museum.
13:00	People-watch and picnic in Retiro Park. Walk to Retiro metro stop. Subway home to siesta.
15:00	Browse, stroll, shop down the Gran Vía to Plaza de España, do Turismo business (free info on all of Spain), ride up to 32nd-floor café for view of Madrid. Explore Puerta del Sol and Plaza Mayor areas.
21:00	Tapas dinner southeast of Puerta del Sol.

Note: Try to be in Madrid on a Sunday for Europe's best flea market, El Rastro, in the morning and a bullfight in the evening. Some Madrid museums, including the Prado and El Escorial, are closed Mondays.

Suggested Schedule Day 2	
8:00	Visit the San Miguel market for breakfast and a browse.
9:00	Be at the Royal Palace when it opens. Tour the palace and its armory.
12:00	**Lunch on Plaza Mayor or near Puerta del Sol, and siesta back home.
14:00	Free afternoon (possible bus or train side trip to El Escorial, which is open until 18:00).

**Those using public transport should go immediately from the Royal Palace to El Escorial. Take advantage of the excellent public transportation connections from downtown Madrid (bus or train, though buses are faster and cheaper than the train). After touring the Royal Palace, walk to the Plaza España metro stop and take the short metro ride to the Monocloa stop. Exit to the left out of the Monocloa metro and you'll walk into the bus stop for El Escorial. Buses leave frequently for El Escorial (640 ptas)—ask about buses to the Valley of the Fallen, and leave Madrid by noon if you want to see this (Autocares Herranz, tel. 543-3645). *Cercanias* (commuter trains) leave frequently from the Atocha station for El Escorial.

By car, visiting these two sights on the way to Segovia is easy.

Orientation—Madrid

Madrid is the hub of Spain. This modern capital, Europe's highest at over 2,000 feet, has a population of over 4 million. It's young by European standards. Only 400 years ago, King Philip II decided to move the capital of his empire from Toledo to Madrid. One hundred years ago, Madrid had only 400,000 people, so nine-tenths of the city is modern sprawl. The historic center can be covered easily on foot. No major sight is more than a fifteen-minute walk from the Puerta del Sol, Madrid's central square.

Today's Madrid is upbeat and vibrant, enjoying a kind of post-Franco renaissance. You'll feel it. It's a proud city that now looks to an exciting future as well as its rich past. As a

Madrid

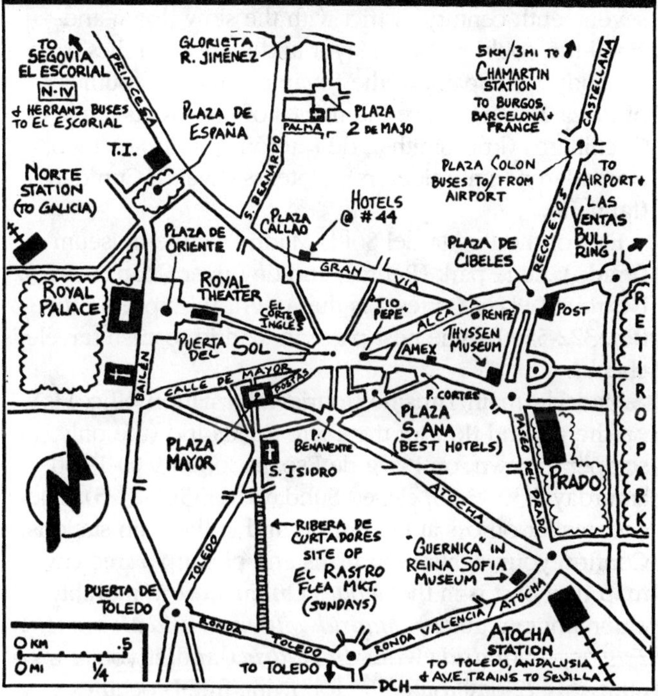

visitor, your time will be divided between the city's two major sights—the palace and the Prado—and its busy bar-hopping, car-honking, sky-scraping contemporary scene.

The Puerta del Sol is at the dead center of Madrid and of Spain itself; notice the kilometer zero marker, from which all of Spain is surveyed, at the police station (southwest corner). The Royal Palace to the west and the Prado Museum and Retiro Park to the east frame the historic center.

North of the palace-Puerta del Sol-Prado line runs the Gran Vía. Between the Gran Vía and the Puerta del Sol are lively pedestrian shopping streets. The Gran Vía, bubbling with business, expensive shops, and cinemas, leads down to the impressively modern Plaza de España. North of the Gran Vía is the fascinating Malasana quarter with its colorful small houses, shoemaker's shops, sleazy-looking *hombres*, milk vendors, bars, and hip night scene.

To the southwest of the Puerta del Sol is an older seventeenth-century district with the slow-down-and-smell-the-cobbles Plaza Mayor and plenty of relics from pre-industrial Spain. In the Lavapies quarter (southeast of Plaza Mayor) notice the names of the streets: Calle de Cuchilleros (knifesmiths), de Laterones (brass-casters), Bordaderos (embroiderers), Tinteros (dyers), Curtideros (tanners).

East of the Puerta del Sol is Madrid's huge museum (Prado), huge park (Retiro), and tiny river (Manzanares). Nearby at Plaza Cortes 2 is the American Express office (tel. 322-5500)—the best place in Madrid to cash traveler's checks.

Madrid's main Turismo (tourist information office) is on the ground floor of the Torre de Madrid (the only sky-scraper in town, on Plaza de España, open 9:00-19:00, Saturday 9:30-13:30, closed Sundays, tel. 541-2325). There are smaller offices at the airport and at the train stations. Confirm your sightseeing plans and pick up a free city map (the best is in the *What's On En Madrid* monthly entertainment guide), *Madrid: Museums and Monuments, Paseos por Madrid (Walks in Madrid)*, and, if you're traveling this 22-day route, the following free brochures: *Toledo, Salamanca, Madrid and Its Surroundings* (for El Escorial), *Segovia, Cuidad Real, Sevilla, Pueblos Blancos of Andalusia, Costa de la Luz* (for Tarifa), *Costa del Sol* (for Nerja), *Granada*, and the amazingly informative *Mapa de Comunicaciones España* listing all the Turismos, Paradores, RENFE train information telephone numbers, and highway SOS numbers with a road map of Spain. Many small town Turismos keep erratic hours and run out of these pamphlets, so get what you can here. Madrid's easy-to-decipher periodical entertainment guide, *Guía del Ocio*, is available at any kiosk.

The U.S. Embassy is at Serrano 75 (tel. 547-4000), and the Canadian Embassy is at Nuñez de Balboa 35 (tel. 431-4000). Madrid's telephone code is 91.

Helpful Hints

Make use of the easy to use subway system (see transportation information under "arrive in Madrid"). Plan ahead. Do what you can in Madrid to smooth out your travel plans. Telephone the day before to confirm your car reservation; ask if they deliver free or how early you can pick up the car. If you're returning to Madrid at the end of your trip, make a reservation at your favorite hotel. Pay in advance so you can arrive as late as you like. You can normally leave anything you won't need in the hotel's storage closet free (mark your name and return date on it clearly). You may also want to reserve rooms now in places where you know exactly where you want to stay and when you'll be there.

Sightseeing Highlights—Madrid

▲▲▲Prado Museum—The Prado is my favorite collection of paintings, anywhere. With over 3,000 paintings, including rooms of masterpieces by Velázquez, Goya, El Greco, and Bosch, it's overwhelming. Take a tour or buy a guidebook (or bring me along by ripping out and packing the Prado chapter from our book, *Mona Winks*). Focus on the Flemish and Northern art (Bosch, Dürer, Rubens); the Italian collection (Fra Angelico, Raphael, Botticelli, Titian); and the Spanish art (El Greco, Velázquez, Goya).

Follow Goya through his cheery (*The Parasol*), political (*The Third of May*), and dark (*Saturn Devouring His Children*) stages. In each stage, Goya asserted his independence from artistic conventions. Even the standard court portraits of his "first" stage reflect his politically liberal viewpoint, subtly showing the vanity and stupidity of his subjects by the look in their goony eyes. His political stage, with paintings like *The Third of May*, depicting a massacre of Spaniards by Napoleon's troops, makes him one of the first artists with a social conscience. Finally, in his gloomy "dark stage," Goya probed the inner world of fears and nightmares, anticipating the twentieth-century preoccupation with dreams. Also, don't miss Bosch's *Garden of Delights*. Most art is grouped by painters and any guard can point you in the right direction if you say *"Donde esta...?"* and the painter's name as Españoled as you can (e.g., Titian is "Ticiano" and Bosch is "El Bosco"). The Prado has a good cafeteria (open 9:00-19:00, Sunday

10:00-14:00, closed Monday, it's quietest at lunchtime—from 14:00 to 15:00, tel. 420-2836, 400 ptas).

▲▲**Picasso's *Guernica***—Located in the Centro de Arte Reina Sofia, three blocks south of the Prado across from the Atocha station, this famous painting showing the horror of modern war deserves much study. The death of Franco ended the work's exile in America, and now it reigns as Spain's national piece of art—behind bulletproof glass. (Tel. 467-5062, open 10:00-21:00, Sundays 10:00-14:30, closed Tuesday, 400 ptas, students free.)

▲**Thyssen-Bornemisza Museum**—This stunning new museum displays the impressive collection of Baron Thyssen (a wealthy German who is married to a former Miss Spain). Art lovers will enjoy the way the good baron's art complements what is in the Prado. Located across from the Prado at Paseo del Prado 8 in the remodeled Palacio de Villahermosa. (Tel. 420-3944, open 10:00-19:00 Tuesday through Sunday, closed Monday, 600 ptas.)

▲▲**Plaza Mayor and Medieval Madrid**—The Plaza Mayor, a vast, cobbled, traffic-free chunk of seventeenth-century Spain is just a short walk from the Puerta del Sol. Each side of the square is uniform, as if a grand palace were turned inside out. Throughout Spain, lesser Plaza Mayors provide peaceful pools for the river of Spanish life. A stamp and coin market bustles here on Sunday mornings, and any day it's a colorful place to enjoy a cup of coffee. (The cafeteria, with a view of the horse's rear, has reasonable "terrace" prices for this great setting, but I wouldn't dine here).

Medieval Madrid is now a rather sterile tangle of narrow streets bounded by the Royal Palace, Plaza Mayor, Teatro Real, and Plaza Puerta de Moros. The uninviting old Plaza de la Villa was the center of Madrid before Madrid was the center of Spain. The most enjoyable action in this area is contained in a glass and iron cage called the Mercado de San Miguel (produce market) next to the Plaza Mayor.

▲▲▲**Palacio Real (Royal Palace)**—Europe's third-greatest palace (after Versailles and Vienna) is packed with tourists and royal antiques. A tour of its clock-filled, rich (but not very graceful) interior is included. English tours go regularly with groups of 10 to 20 (500 ptas, Monday-Saturday 9:30-17:15, Sunday 9:00-14:15, tel. 559-7404; very crowded in summer, arrive early or at lunch). Your ticket includes the equally impressive armory and the pharmacy, both on the courtyard. The nearby Museo de Carruajes Reales has an impressive collection of royal carriages.

▲Zarzuela—For a delightful look at Spanish light opera that even English-speakers can enjoy, try an evening of Zarzuela. Guitar-strumming Napoleons in red capes, buxom women with masks and fans, castanets and stomping feet, aficionados singing along from the cheap seats where the acoustics and cleavages are best, Spanish-speaking pharaohs, melodramatic spotlights, bullfight music with legions of glittering matadors—that's Zarzuela. The *What's On En Madrid* periodical has a special Zarzuela listing. You might also check the Teatro de la Zarzuela (tel. 429-1286, metro: Banco de España). Don't mess with flamenco in Madrid. Save yourself for Seville.

▲▲El Rastro—Europe's biggest flea market is a field day for people-watchers (Sundays from 9:00-12:00, best early). Thousands of stalls titillate over a million browsers. If you brake for garage sales, you'll pull a U-turn for El Rastro. You can buy or sell nearly anything here. Start at the Plaza Mayor and head south, or take the subway to Tirso de Molina. Hang onto your wallet. Munch on a sweet *pepito* (sweet pudding-filled pastry) or a *relleno.* Europe's biggest stamp market thrives simultaneously on the Plaza Mayor.

▲Chapel San Antonio de la Florida—Goya's tomb stares up at a splendid cupola filled with his own frescoes (Tuesday-Friday 9:00-14:00 and 16:00-20:00, Saturday and Sunday 10:00-13:00, closed Monday, free, tel. 547-7921).

▲▲Retiro Park—Siesta in this 350-acre green and breezy escape from the city. Rent a rowboat, have a picnic. These peaceful gardens offer great people-watching. The Botanical Garden (Jardín Botánico) nearby is a pleasant extension of Retiro Park to the southwest. Ride the metro to Retiro, walk to the big lake (El Estanque) where you can rent a rowboat, or wander through the Palacio de Crystal. A grand boulevard of statues leads to the Prado.

▲▲▲Bullfight—Madrid's Plaza de Toros hosts Spain's top bullfights on most Sundays and holidays from Easter through October. Top fights sell out in advance, but you can generally get a ticket at the door. Fights usually start at 19:00 or 20:00 and are a rare example of Spanish punctuality. There are no bad seats; paying more gets you in the shade and/or closer to the gore (filas 8, 9, and 10 tend to be closest to the action). You can buy tickets (800 to 5,000 ptas) at C. de la Victoria 1, between the Puerta del Sol and the Plaza Santa Ana on Pl. del Carmen 1 (tel. 431-2732) and, cheapest, at the bullring. Madrid and Sevilla will probably be your only chances to catch a bullfight in Spain on this tour. The bullfighting museum (Museo Taurino) is next to the bullring (daily 9:00-14:00, metro: Ventas, tel. 356-2200, free). See the Appendix for more on the "art" of bullfighting.

▲▲Plaza de España—Modern Madrid centers around this plaza with its huge stone monument to Cervantes (with statues of Don Quixote and Sancho Panza), plenty of busy student-filled cafés, and the Madrid tower or skyscraper, which offers a great city view from its 32nd-floor café (Monday-Friday 9:30-21:30, Saturday 13:00-15:30, closed Sunday, 100 ptas or free if you buy a drink). Note: the city's best Turismo and the RENFE office are in this skyscraper.

▲Real Fabrica de Tapices (Royal Tapestry Factory) offers a look at the traditional making of tapestries (cheap tours in Spanish only, open Monday-Friday 9:30-12:30, closed August, metro: Menendez Pelayo, tel. 551-3400, 50 ptas).

▲Paseo—The people of Madrid ("Madrileños") siesta because so much goes on in the evening. The nightly paseo is Madrid on parade. Young and old, everyone's outside taking a stroll, "cruising" without cars, seeing and being seen. Gran Vía and the Paseo del Prado are particularly active scenes.

Parque de Atracciones—For a colorful amusement park scene, complete with Venetian canals, dancing, eating, games, free shows, and top-notch people-watching, try Parque de Atracciones (open most afternoons and

evenings until around midnight, only Saturday and Sunday in off-season, tel. 463-2900 for exact times, metro: Batań) This fun fair and Spain's best zoo (open 10:00-21:00) are both in the vast Casa del Campo Park just west of the Royal Palace.
Shopping—Shoppers can focus on the colorful pedestrian area between Gran Vía and Puerta del Sol. Those born to shop may want to drop by the elegant new shopping mall across the street from the Prado, La Galería del Prado (decent self-service La Plaza cafeteria inside).

Sleeping in Madrid, telephone code: 91, postal code for central Madrid: 28070.
Madrid has plenty of centrally located budget hotels and pensions. From the Puerta del Sol, wander generally south and east. Doorbells line each building entrance. Push one that says "Pensión." You'll have no trouble finding a decent double for $25 to $50.

Reminder: this book's hotel double-room price categories are very cheap—under $17; cheap—under $26; inexpensive—$26 to $45; moderate—$45 to $65; expensive—over $65. Most guidebooks list the modern hotels, with much higher prices than my most expensive listing.
If your money is limited, don't judge a place by its dreary entryway. Madrid is most crowded in July and August, but it's never really tough to find a place. The rooms get cheaper—and seedier—as you approach the Atocha station. Here are some hotels clustered in three particularly good areas.

Rooms on Gran Vía: (postal code: 28013) The pulse of today's Madrid is best felt along the Gran Vía. This big, busy main drag in the heart of the city stays light all night. Even with the sex theaters, there's a certain urban decency about it. The best hotels lie across from Plaza del Callão, a colorful four blocks of pedestrian malls up from the Puerta del Sol. While many rooms are high above the traffic noise, I'd ask for a brick wall view from a quiet room on the back side. All my Gran Vía choices are in the nine floors of Gran Vía #44; the entrance is between the Lladro shop and the Loteria, (postal code: 28013 Madrid). The elevator is smelly but a big help and the well-lit corridor is

Heart of Madrid

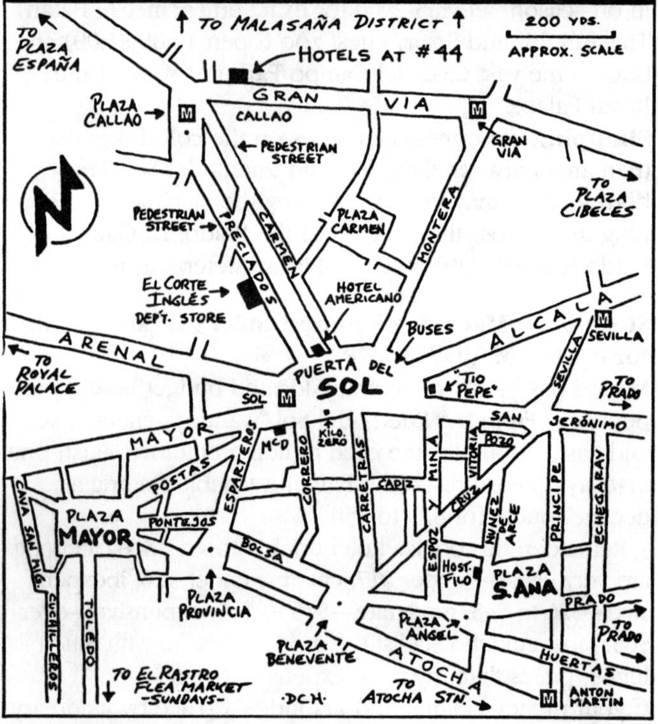

so quiet you can hear the sound of spit hitting the ground from eight floors up. The fancy old Café Fuyma next door (corner of C. de Miguel Moya and Gran Vía) provides a classy way to breakfast. The Callão metro stop is at your doorstep.

Hostal Residencia Miami is clean, quiet, and cheery, with lovely well-lit rooms (splitting the molded ceilings of its glory days when rooms were larger), padded doors, and plastic flower decor throughout. It's like staying at your eccentric aunt's in Miami Beach. The bubbly landlady, Mrs. Sanz, and her careful husband, who dresses up each day for work here, are patient and friendly but speak very little English (cheap-inexpensive, Gran Vía #44, eighth floor, tel. 521-1464, closed August).

Across the hall is **Hostal Alibel**, Miami without the sugar. It's big, airy, and quiet (inexpensive, tel. 521-0051).

Downstairs, **Hostal Josefina** smells like fish, has creaky vinyl floors and junkyard doors but strong beds in museum-warehouse rooms (cheap singles and doubles with showers, Gran Vía 44, 7th floor, tel. 521-8131 and 531-0466, no English spoken...ever).

Hostal Residencia Valencia is bright, cheery, and much more professional than the others. The friendly manager, Antonio Ramirez, speaks English (inexpensive, all with shower and W.C., Gran Vía 44, 6th floor, tel. 522-1115 and 522-1114). Also friendly and a good value but below Valencia in every way but price is **Hostal Residencia Continental** (inexpensive, 4th floor, tel. 521-4640 and 521-4649).

Rooms on Plaza Santa Ana: The Plaza Santa Ana area has plenty of small, pleasant, and cheap places. It's my favorite Madrid locale for its almost Parisian ambience, colorful bars, and very central location—three minutes past the Puerta del Sol's "Tío Pepe" sign: walk down C. San Jeronimo and make a right on Principe. A great breakfast hangout is Restaurante Gerva (around the corner a block toward Puerta del Sol where Calle de Alvarez Gato hits Calle de la Cruz, open from 7:00, closed Sunday). The whole area between there and Puerta del Sol is tapa heaven for your pub crawl dining pleasure (see below). Postal code: 28012 Madrid. Metro: Sol.

Hostal Filo is squeaky clean with a nervous but helpful management and a confusing floor plan. No English is spoken. (Inexpensive, Plaza de Santa Ana 15, second floor, tel. 522-4056, closed August.)

Hostal Delvi, upstairs on the 3rd floor, is also bright, clean and friendly (inexpensive doubles; four bright, cheap singles with shower; tel. 522-5998, no English spoken). Also on the third floor is the dreary but sleepable **Hostal la Rosa** (inexpensive, tel. 532-7046).

A few yards toward the Puerta del Sol is **Hostal Lucense** offering very basic rooms, none with private showers, and hardworking English-speaking managers, Sr. and Sra. Muñoz (cheap, Nuñez de Arce 15, tel. 522-4888). They also run the neighboring and similar **Casa Huéspedes Poza** (Nuñez de Arce 9, tel. 222-4871). Not far from the Plaza Santa is the newly redone Pension Asturias on Calle Atocha 3, tel. 369-2871.

Easy-to-please vagabonds might enjoy playing corkscrew up the rickety cut-glass elevator to **Pensión La Valenciana** with very old and funky rooms, some with balconies over the square and one with a great corner location (cheap, Principe 27, 4th floor, right on Plaza Santa Ana next to the theater, tel. 429-6317, no English spoken). Rock bottom in this area is the acceptable **Hostal Residencia Canal** (very cheap doubles and singles, one block off the square at Huertas 4, tel. 429-1859, no English).

Rooms near Puerta del Sol and Plaza Mayor: Hostal Montalvo is just 85 cobbles off the elegant Plaza Mayor on a quiet and traffic-free street up a well-worn and dark stairway (no elevator) and run by English-speaking Lucia and Alejandro and their parents (inexpensive doubles and singles, Zaragoza 6, 3rd floor, 28012 Madrid, tel. 365-5910) Reasonable breakfast places are right on the Plaza Mayor.

The hotels on the Puerta del Sol are generally dingy. If you must look out over the heartbeat of Madrid, try the smoky, stuffy **Hostal Residencia Americano**, with a mean owner whose neck shakes like a turkey's when he says "No" as you sneak a photo of the square from his lobby balcony (moderate, choose quiet in back or view in front, Puerta del Sol 11, tel. 522-2822).

Rooms near the Prado: Two very good values in a modern building are just across from the Prado Museum. **Hotel Sud-Americana** (inexpensive, Paseo del Prado 12, sixth floor, tel. 429-2564) and **Hostal Residencia Coruña** (inexpensive, Paseo del Prado 12, third floor, tel. 429-2543) are clean and friendly, though they come with some traffic noise and are filled with Frommer and *Let's Go* readers. The staff speaks enough English.

Youth Hostels: Madrid has two good youth hostels. **Santa Cruz de Marcenado** (Calle Santa Cruz de Marcenado 28, tel. 247-4532), near metro stop Arguelles, is clean and well run, in a student neighborhood, cheap, but has a 0:30 curfew. There's also youth hostel **Richard Schirrman** (in the dangerous-at-night Casa de Campo, tel. 463-5699) near metro stop El Lago. Since hotels and hostales (Spanish-style hotels, not to be confused with youth hostels) are so inexpensive in Madrid, I'd skip the youth hostels. If you're on a real tight budget, find a dingy 1,500 ptas double around Plaza Santa Ana.

Eating in Madrid

Madrid loves to eat well. In Spain, only Barcelona rivals Madrid for taste bud thrills. You have two basic dining choices: an atmospheric sit-down meal in a well-chosen restaurant or tapas in a bar.

Near the Plaza Santa Ana is the restaurant Pozo Real (C. Del Pozo 6, tel. 521 7951). It's mucho friendly, popular with the locals and very reasonable. Meander to the back for quieter tables. Next door is Madrid's best pastry shop.

Historic **Lhardy**, near Puerta del Sol at Carrera de San Jeronimo 8, has great tapas downstairs. For a splurge, climb into the classy nineteenth-century atmosphere upstairs.

The meals are hearty and tasty, the TV is on, and the locals know each other at **Restaurante Rodriguez** (750 pta menu, 15 San Cristobal, one block toward Sol from Plaza Mayor, tel. 231-1136). Restaurants don't get crowded until after 22:00.

Most Americans are drawn to Hemingway's favorite, **Sobrinos del Botín** (Cuchilleros 17 in old town, 266-4217). Frighteningly touristy, it's the last place he'd go now.

For a potentially more atmospheric mobile meal, do the popular "tapa tango"—a local tradition of going from one bar to the next, munching, drinking, and socializing. Tapas are small toothpick appetizers, salads, and deep-fried foods served in most bars. Dinners in Madrid are not cheap. Tapas are, and Madrid is Spain's tapa capital. Grab a toothpick and stab something strange.

A good tapas district is the area between Puerta del Sol and Plaza Santa Ana. For tapa bars, try this route: from Puerta del Sol, head east along Carrera de San Jeronimo, then branch off onto Calles de la Cruz and Nuñez del Arce. At Carrera San Jeronimo 6, poke into the Museo del Jamón ("Museum of Ham"—note the tasty decor, with well-cured smoked ham and sausage lining the ceiling). This is a frenetic, cheap, stand-up bar with an assembly line of fast and deliciously simple bocadillos and raciones. Shrimp lovers should seek out the tiny La Casa del Abuelo on Victoria 12, where sizzling *gambas* go down great with the house wine.

A perfect place to assemble a cheap picnic is downtown Madrid's neighborhood market, Mercado de San Miguel, in the Plaza Mayor. Face the colorful building and exit from the upper left hand corner. How about breakfast in the market's café/bar surrounded by early morning shoppers, and a couple of delicious oranges to go? El Corte Ingles has a well-stocked deli.

Each night the Malasana quarter around the Plaza Dos de Mayo erupts with street life. Madrid's bohemian, intellectual, liberal scene has flowered since the death of Franco. Artists, actors, former exiles, and Madrid's youth gather here. Single women should probably carry Mace and a whistle.

DAY 3

EL ESCORIAL, VALLEY OF THE FALLEN, AND SEGOVIA

Pick up your rental car or catch the train. Don't leave Madrid without a map of Segovia and Salamanca, available at Madrid's Turismos. Drivers will head for the countryside to tour the brutal but fascinating Escorial palace and the awesome underground memorial basilica dedicated to the victims of Spain's bloody Civil War, while those on the train will go directly to Segovia. Set up in Segovia with time to enjoy its old center, cathedral, and castle. By dinnertime, you'll be hungry enough to eat an entire roast suckling pig. Do so. Busy day. Tasty finale.

Suggested Schedule—By Car

9:00	Pick up rental car and drive northwest.
10:00	Tour El Escorial. Lunch in town there or buy a picnic for Valley of the Fallen.
14:00	Tour Valley of the Fallen memorial to victims of Spain's Civil War.
16:00	Drive an hour to Segovia; check into hotel.
18:00	Stroll down to aqueduct.
20:00	Roast suckling pig for dinner.

Note: Train travelers may do El Escorial as a morning side trip, skip Valley of the Fallen, return to Madrid, and take the train directly to Segovia.

The Route: Madrid to Segovia (50 miles)

Take a taxi to your car rental office. Pick up the car by 8:30 and ask directions to highway A6. From the airport, drive back into town. Follow A6-Valladolid signs to the clearly marked exit on M505 to El Escorial. Get to El Escorial by 9:30 to beat the crowds.

From El Escorial, follow C600 Valle de los Caídos signs to the Valley of the Fallen. You'll see the huge cross marking it in the distance. After the toll booth, follow basilica signs to the parking place (toilets, tacky souvenirs, and

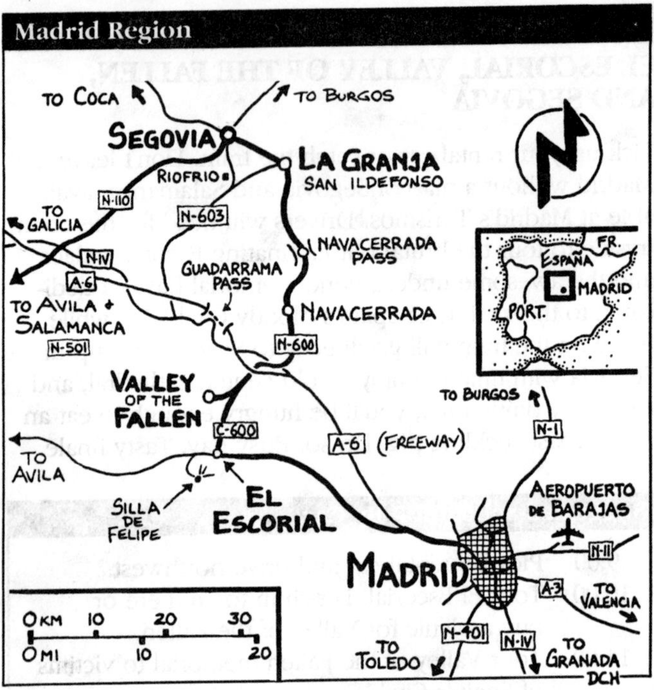

cafeteria). As you leave, turn left to Guadarrama on C600, go under the highway, follow signs to Pto. de Navacerrada. From there, you climb past flocks of sheep, over a 6,000-foot-high mountain pass (Puerto de Navacerrada) into old Castile, through La Granja to Segovia. (Today is already jam-packed, and Segovia is much more important than La Granja, but if you're into gardens you might want to squeeze in a quick La Granja stop.)

At the Segovia aqueduct, turn into the old town (the side where the aqueduct adjoins the crenellated fortress walls) and park as close to the Plaza Mayor as possible. . . ideally, on it. Parking in Segovia is no picnic. Ideally, grab a spot on the Plaza Mayor in front of the cathedral. To be legal, and they do issue expensive tickets, pick up a cheap permit from the Tobac shop just down C.I. Católica (90 minutes maximum between 9:00 and 20:00).

By Bus and Train

Regular bus and train departures connect Madrid and Segovia. Don't leave the station in Segovia without tomorrow's schedules. Trains take about 2 hours and leave from Madrid's Chamartin station. Look for the *Cercanias* (commuter train) ticket window and departure board and get the return schedule to Madrid. Buses take an hour and a half and depart from La Sepulvedana bus station (Metro Norte stop, Po. de al Florida, 3). In Segovia, take city bus # 2 or #3 from the train station to the Pl. Mayor (75 ptas, the stop is to the right as you leave the station, near side). If you arrive by bus, take bus #3, or even better, walk to the center: turn right out of the bus station and left onto C. Ladrera. Taxis are a reasonable option.

Sightseeing Highlights near Madrid

▲▲▲El Escorial—The Monasterio de San Lorenzo de El Escorial is a symbol of power rather than elegance. This sixteenth-century palace, 30 miles northwest of Madrid, gives us a better feel for the Counter-Reformation and the Inquisition than any other building. Built at a time when Catholic Spain felt threatened by Protestant "heretics," its construction dominated the Spanish economy for 20 years. For that reason, Spain has almost nothing else to show from this most powerful period of her history. The giant, gloomy building (gray-black stone, 2,500 windows, 1,000 doors, over 100 miles of passages, 200 yards long and 150 yards wide) looks more like a prison than a palace. Four hundred years ago, the enigmatic and introverted King Philip II ruled his bulky empire and directed the Inquisition from here. To sixteenth-century followers of Luther, this place epitomized the evil of Catholicism. It's been said that if Spain was a cathedral, this would be its choir (*coro*), packed with history, art, and Inquisition ghosts.

El Escorial is confusing, but guides in each room can answer questions. See the church (free, put 100 ptas in the light box for a spectacular illumination), mausoleum (stacked with 26 royal tombs), and monastery with the royal palace and the austere private apartments of intriguing King Philip II. You'll see magnificent tapestries made from Goya paintings you saw in the Prado, and a great library with a thousand-year-old book of the Gospels printed with 17 pounds of gold leaf letters, each cut out and pasted on with egg-white glue. The Museos Nuevos (New Museums) have some impressive paintings, including works by El Greco, Bosch, and Titian (500 ptas, open 10:00-18:00, closed Monday, tel. 890-5011).

To shop for a picnic, stop by the Mercado Publico on C. del Rey 9, a four-minute walk from the palace (9:00-14:00, closed Thursday and Sunday).

If you are driving, check out the nearby Silla de Felipe (Philip's Seat), a rocky viewpoint where the king would come to admire his palace.

▲▲▲El Valle de los Caídos (Valley of the Fallen)—Five miles toward Segovia from El Escorial, high in the Guadarrama Mountains, towers a 150-yard-tall granite cross. This is just the tip of the memorial iceberg, marking an immense and powerful underground monument to the countless victims of Spain's twentieth-century nightmare—its Civil War (1936-1939). A solemn silence fills the memorial room, larger (860 feet long) than St. Peter's Basilica, as Spaniards pass under the huge forbidding angels of Fascism to visit the grave of General Franco. Notice the eight sixteenth-century Brussels tapestries of the Apocalypse and the alabaster copies of the most famous Virgin Mary statues in Spain in each chapel. The term "basilica" is normally used for a church built over the remains of a saint, not a fascist dictator. Even though 40,000 bodies are resting here, Franco is center stage, and it was his prisoners, the enemies of the right, who dug this memorial. On your way out, stare into the eyes of those angels with swords and two right wings and think about all the "heroes" who keep dying "for God and country," at the request of the latter (350 ptas, open 10:00-18:00, closed Monday, funicular to the cross 10:00-13:00, 14:30-17:30).

▲La Granja Palace—This "Little Versailles," six miles south of Segovia, is much smaller and happier than El Escorial. The palace and gardens were built by the homesick French king, Philip V, grandson of Louis XIV. It's a must for tapestry lovers. Fountain displays (which send local crowds into a frenzy) erupt at 17:30 on most Thursdays, Saturdays, Sundays, and holidays. Entry to the palace includes a required 45-minute guided tour (English rare). Ten buses a day make the 30-minute trip from Segovia (admission 400 ptas, open 10:00-18:00, closed Monday).

Segovia Orientation

Segovia (elevation 3,000 ft., population 55,000, 50 miles from Madrid) boasts a great Roman aqueduct, a cathedral, and a castle. Segovia is a medieval "ship" ready for your inspection. Start at the stern—the aqueduct—and stroll up Calle de Cervantes to the prickly Gothic masts of the cathedral. Explore the tangle of narrow streets around the Plaza Mayor, then descend to the Alcázar at the bow.

There are two helpful tourist offices in Segovia, the most convenient of which is at Plaza Mayor 10 (open 10:00-14:00, 16:30-19:00, closed Saturday afternoon and Sunday, tel. 911/43 03 28; the other is under the aqueduct, near the steps. Need a map of Ávila or Salamanca?). Train information: 42 07 74 or 42 63 38. Telephone code: 911.

Sightseeing Highlights—Segovia

▲Roman Aqueduct—Built by the Romans, who ruled Spain for over 500 years, this 2,000-year-old *acueducto Romano* is 2,500 feet long and 100 feet high, has 118 arches, was made without any mortar, and it still works. It's considered Segovia's backup plumbing. From underneath the aqueduct, walk up the steps for the best view.

▲Cathedral—Segovia's cathedral was Spain's last major Gothic building. Embellished to the hilt with pinnacles and flying buttresses, this is a great example of the final overripe stage of Gothic called "Flamboyant." The spacious and elegant but dark interior provides a delightful contrast (admission is free; 200 ptas gets you into the small but interesting museum and the cloister. Open 9:00-19:00).

▲▲Alcázar—This Disneyesque rebuilt exaggeration of the old castle, which burned down 100 years ago, is still fun to explore and worthwhile for the view of Segovia

Segovia

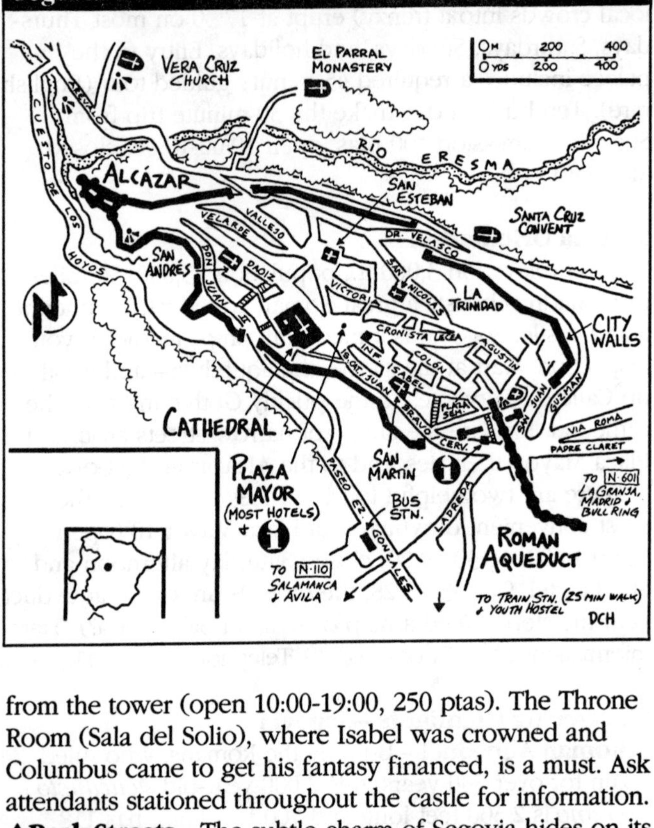

from the tower (open 10:00-19:00, 250 ptas). The Throne Room (Sala del Solio), where Isabel was crowned and Columbus came to get his fantasy financed, is a must. Ask attendants stationed throughout the castle for information.

▲Back Streets—The subtle charm of Segovia hides on its back streets. Its Romanesque churches are usually open only for services (daily around 8:00 and 19:00). Try resurrecting old Segovia this way: visit Iglesia de la Trinidad with its simple, dark, hotline-to-heaven interior, step into the old courtyard at #8 across the street (fortified wall, old wooden ceiling beams), and have a beer or coffee in the Bar Los Campo.

Front Streets—don't miss a stroll up or down the pleasant shopping street, Calle Juan Bravo, which connects the Plaza Mayor and the aqueduct. Here you can pick up a picnic, join the evening paseo and rub shoulders with Segovian yuppies.

▲**Vera Cruz church**—This 12-sided, thirteenth-century Romanesque church was built by the Knights Templar and used to house a piece of the "true cross" (open 10:30-13:30 and 15:30-19:00, closed Monday, 125 ptas). There's a postcard city view from here (especially from the church's tower), and more views follow as you continue around Segovia on the "ruta turistica panoramica."

Sleeping in Segovia, telephone code: 911, postal code 40006.

The best places are on or near the central Plaza Mayor (still called Plaza de Franco on some tourist maps). This is where the city action is: the cheapest and best bars, most touristic and *típico* eateries, and the Turismo. Parking is free from 20:00 to 9:00 and safe on the square. Postal code: 40006 Segovia. In Spain, dialing 911 gets you Segovia, not emergency.

Hostal Residencia Plaza (inexpensive, Cronista Lecea 11, tel. 43 12 28 and 44 02 44) is very central, just off Plaza Mayor toward the aqueduct. You'll find serioso management, long snaky corridors, and furniture carefully tied down, but it's clean and cozy.

Right on the square at #4 are two tiny, dark, but clean enough places (look hard for the Hospedale Habitaciones sign). Both are kind of like staying with grandparents who don't get out much anymore. **Pensión Aragon** (two very cheap doubles hiding past tunnels of dark wallpaper on the first floor, tel. 43 35 27) is a bit better than **Casa de Huéspedes Cubo** (also very cheap, second floor, tel. 43 63 86). Places this cheap never speak English.

Hotel Los Linajes (expensive, at Dr. Valasco 9, tel. 43 12 01) is ultra-classy, with rusticity mixed into its newly poured concrete. This poor-man's parador is a few blocks beyond the Plaza Mayor (follow the small signs) just past San Esteban church, with commanding views and modern niceties, parking, and even a disco bar. A place I don't like which fills a void in Segovia is the big, stuffy, hotel-esque **Hotel Sirenas** (moderate, three blocks down from the Pl. Mayor at C. Juan Bravo 30, tel. 43 40 11).

Right across from the train station is the **Hostal Sol Cristina** (cheap, C. Obispo Quesada 40, tel. 42 75 13), and nearby is the **Hostal Residencia Sol Cristina-Dos** (inexpensive, Carretera de Villacastin, 6, tel. 42 75 13).

The **Segovia Youth Hostel** (on Paseo Conde de Sepulveda between the train and bus stations, tel. 42 02 26, open only in July and August) is a great hostel—easygoing, comfortable, clean, friendly, and very cheap. Segovia is crowded in July and August, so arrive early or call ahead.

Eating in Segovia

Roast suckling pig (*cochinillo asado*, 21 days of mother's milk, into the oven, and onto your plate), Segovia's culinary claim to fame, is worth a splurge here (or in Toledo or Salamanca). While you're at it, try the *sopa Castellana.*

The **Mesón de Candido** (Plaza del Azoguejo 3, under the aqueduct, tel. 42 81 03 for reservations) is one of the top restaurants in Castile—famous, good, and worth the splurge if you'd like to spend 2,500 ptas on a memorable dinner. Plenty good, just off the Plaza Mayor, and even more típico is **La Oficina** (Cronista Lecea 10, tel. 43 16 43). **Narizotas** (1 Plaza de Medina del Campo, tel. 43 46 37), attracts locals with lots of delicious *platos combinados* at fair prices.

The cheapest bars and eateries line Calle de Infanta Isabel just off the Plaza Mayor. For nightlife, the bars on Plaza Mayor and Calles Infanta Isabel and Isabel la Católica are packed. Stop by the **Povi** shop (just off the square on Calle Lecea) for 200 grams of homemade potato chips. The cafeteria bar **Korppus** (Plaza del Corpus, a block down C. I. Católica from the Plaza Mayor, look for blue awnings) is my breakfast choice. There's no real supermarket in the old town, but an outdoor produce market thrives around Plaza de los Huertos Thursdays from 8:00 to 14:00.

DAY 4

SEGOVIA AND SALAMANCA

After a morning in Segovia's romantic castle and musty cathedral, you'll travel two hours to Spain's university town, Salamanca. College-town frisky, Salamanca has Spain's best Plaza Mayor, unique architecture, a feisty history, and the world's biggest communion wafers.

Suggested Schedule	
9:00	Tour Segovia's Cathedral, then the Alcázar.
12:00	Drive to Salamanca.
14:00	Set up in Salamanca, tour university, cathedrals, and convents, and enjoy Plaza Mayor.

The Route: Segovia to Salamanca (100 miles)
Leave Segovia by driving around the town's circular road, which offers good views from below the Alcázar. Then follow the signs for Ávila (road N110). Notice the fine town view from the three crosses at the crest of the first hill. Just after the abandoned ghost church at Villacastin, turn onto N501 at the huge Puerta de San Vicente (cathedral and Turismo are just inside). The Salamanca road leads around the famous Ávila walls to the right. The best wall view is from the signposted "Cuatro Postes," a mile northwest of town. Salamanca (N501) is clearly marked, about an hour's drive away.

A few miles before Salamanca you might want to stop at the huge bull on the right of the road. There's a little dirt path leading right up to it. The closer you get, the more you realize it isn't real. Bad boys enjoy climbing it for a goofy photo, but I wouldn't. At the edge of Salamanca, at the light before the first bridge, you'll have a great photo opportunity complete with river reflection.

Parking in Salamanca is terrible. You can park over the river or along the Paseo de Canaliejas for free. I found a meter near my hotel (along C. Palominos) and kept it fed (100 ptas for two hours, 9:00-14:00, 16:00-20:00, free

Saturday and Sunday afternoon). This is a headache, but it's safer. Leave nothing of value in your car.

By Bus and Train

The most direct route to Salamanca is via bus and takes about 2 hours. With only three trips a day you should verify schedules. Train riders must return early to Madrid's Chamartin station to catch the mid-morning (about 9:30) departure to Salamanca, a 6-hour trip. Train riders have an interesting option upon arrival in Salamanca about 13:00: check their bags at Salamanca's station and sightsee until about 2:00 a.m., then catch a peaceful night train to Coimbra—olé!! The train and bus stations in Salamanca are an easy bus ride or a 20-minute walk to the Plaza Mayor. From the train station, turn left out of the station and walk down to the ring road, cross it, then angle up C. Azafranal, (train information: tel. 22 57 42 or 21 24 54). From the bus station, turn right and walk down Ave. Filiberto Villobos then up Ramon y Cajal (bus info: 23 76 17). Get schedules for tomorrow.

Ávila

A popular side trip from Madrid, this town, the birthplace of St. Teresa, has perfectly preserved medieval walls (to climb onto them, enter through the gardens of the parador) and several fine churches and monasteries. Pick up a box of the famous local sweets called *yemas*—like a soft-boiled egg yolk cooled and sugared.

Salamanca

This sunny sandstone city boasts Spain's grandest Plaza Mayor, its oldest university, a strolling college-town ambience, and a fascinating history that is fun to absorb. There are two Turismos to choose from: the more convenient is on the Pl. Mayor, at 3 o'clock as you face the clock, under the arch; the other is next to the cathedral (just inside the Puerta de San Vicente). Both are open, 9:00-14:00, 17:00-19:00, closed Saturday and Sunday afternoons (tel. 21 13 87). Telephone code: 923.

Sightseeing Highlights—Salamanca

▲▲▲Plaza Mayor—Built in 1755, this is the ultimate Spanish plaza. It's a fine place to nurse a cup of coffee, watch the world go by, and imagine the excitement of the days, just a hundred years ago, when bullfights were held here. How about coffee at the town's oldest café, Café Novelty?

▲▲Cathedrals, Old and New—The two cathedrals, both richly ornamented, share buttresses. You get to the old through the new. Before entering, check out the ornate Plateresque facade (Spain's version of Flamboyant Gothic). The "new" cathedral was begun in 1513, with Renaissance and baroque parts added later (free and lack-luster). Enter the old (twelfth-century) cathedral from near the rear of the new one (9:00-14:00, 16:00-18:00, closed Sunday afternoon, 200 ptas). Sit in a front pew to study the 53 scenes from the altarpiece of Mary's life (*retablo*) and the Last Judgment fresco above it. Then head into the cloister and explore each of the chapels. Capilla San Bartolome (de Los Anajas) has what might be the oldest church organ anywhere (1380) and a gorgeously carved sixteenth-century tomb.

▲▲University—Salamanca University is the oldest in Spain (1230) and was one of Europe's leading centers of learning for 400 years. Columbus came here for some travel advice, and today many Americans enjoy its excellent summer program (entrance is off C. Libreros, open 9:30-13:30, 16:30-18:30, Sundays from 10:00-13:00, 150 ptas. Buy the English info sheet, 15 ptas). Explore the old lecture halls around the cloister where many of Spain's Golden Age heroes studied.

In the Hall of Fray Luis de León, sit on a bench at the rough table whittled down by centuries of studious doodling and imagine the lecturer in his church-threatening *catedra*, or pulpit. It was here that freethinking Fray Luis de León, after the Inquisition imprisoned and tortured him for five years, returned to his place and started his first post-jail lecture with, "As we were saying yesterday. . . ."

Compare the truthful simplicity of this decor to the Churrigueresque in the churriurch. The entrance portal is

Salamanca

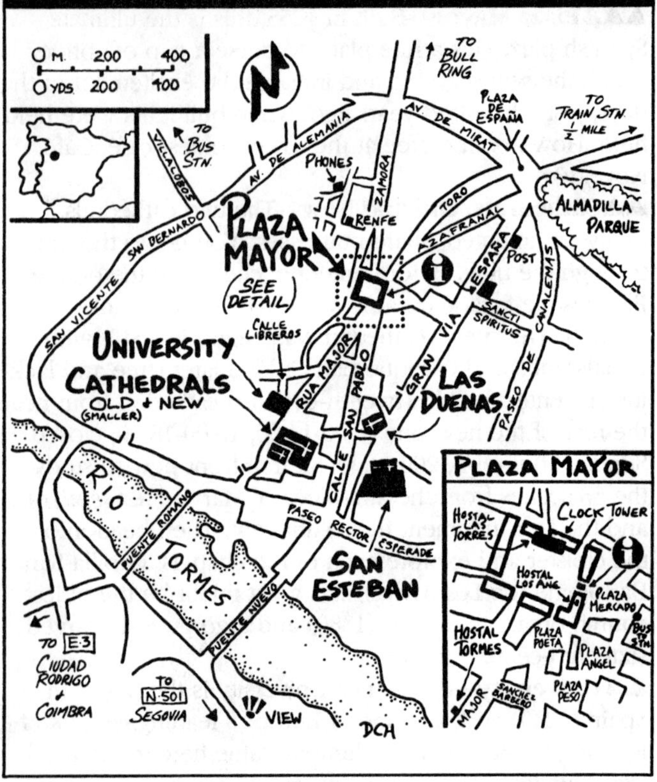

a great example of Spain's Plateresque style—masonry so intricate it looks like silver work. Everybody is trying to find a tiny frog that students looked to for good luck. I know where it is, but it was so hard to find, I'll let you search. (Hint: it's on the forehead of a skull.)

Convento de San Esteban and Convento de las Dueñas—These two famous convents are rich in art and history but not required sightseeing. Both are just a few blocks from the cathedral. The Convento de San Esteban's Plateresque facade is worth a look and inside is a Churriguera altarpiece, a textbook example of the style that is named after him. Sit in a pew and listen to tourists retch as they say "too much" in their mother tongue. After all this gold-plated cottage cheese, the much simpler

Dominican Convento de las Dueñas, next door, is a joy. Check out the little stone meanies decorating the capitals on the cloister's upper deck (both convents open 10:00-13:00, 16:00-17:30 daily, Esteban until 19:00).

Sleeping and Eating in Salamanca, telephone code: 923, postal code: 37002.
Salamanca, being a student town, has plenty of good eating and sleeping values. Getting a decent room right where you want it should be easy. All my listings are on or within a three-minute walk of the Plaza Mayor; directions are given from the Plaza Mayor assuming you are facing the building with the clock (e.g., 3 o'clock is 90 degrees to your right as you face the clock).

Hostal Los Angeles (at about 3 o'clock, cheap, Plaza Mayor 10, tel. 21 81 66), which has simple but cared-for rooms overlooking the square, is run by Louis and Sabina. Stand on your balcony and inhale the essence of Spain. A regal on-the-square option is **Hotel Las Torres** (under the clock, expensive, Plaza Mayor 47, tel. 21 21 00, fax. 21 22 01).

Hotel Milan (leave the Pl. Mayor at about 5 o'clock and walk 2 blocks down, inexpensive, Plaza del Angel 5, 37001 Salamanca, tel. 21 75 18) is your best normal hotel budget bet with a friendly yet professional atmosphere, a TV lounge, and quiet rooms. The clean and homey **Hostal La Perla Salmantina** (exit Pl. Mayor at about 6 o'clock and walk down the Rua Mayor, then left to Sánchez Barbero 7, tel. 21 76 56) is a cozy gem in an ideal, quiet location. The quiet and handy **Hostal Tormes** (see above hotel for directions, cheap, Rua Mayor 20, tel. 21 96 83) is a student-type residence with big, clean, spartan rooms on the pedestrian street connecting the Plaza Mayor and the University.

There are plenty of good, inexpensive restaurants between the Plaza Mayor and the Gran Vía and as you leave the Pl. Mayor toward the Rua Mayor. Just wander and eat at your own discovery or try **Café Novelty** (Plaza Mayor's oldest coffee shop), **Mesón de Cervantes** (Plaza Mayor, good tapas, sit outside or upstairs), the very local

La Covachuela (under the Pl. Mayor on Plaza Mercado 24), and several places on Calle Bermejeros (like **Taberna de Pilatos** and **De la Reina**). The covered mercado on Pl. Mercado is ideal for picnic gatherers.

And if you always wanted seconds at communion, don't leave town without buying a bag of giant communion wafers, a local specialty called *obleas*.

DAY 5

SALAMANCA TO COIMBRA, PORTUGAL

Today we'll say adiós to Spain's "City of Grace," Salamanca, explore the medieval turrets and crannies of Ciudad Rodrigo, and cross into Portugal to set up in its prestigious university town of Coimbra. You'll gain an hour in your favor today if it's daylight savings season.

Suggested Schedule—By Car	
8:00	Early start, late breakfast in Cuidad Rodrigo?
13:00	Arrive in Coimbra, set up, and lunch.
15:00	Tour the university and old cathedral and browse the old quarter.

The Route: Salamanca to Coimbra (210 miles)/ Salamanca to Ciudad Rodrigo (60 miles): An easy 6-hour drive.

Ciudad Rodrigo to Coimbra (150 miles): The drive is fast, easy, uncrowded and, until Guarda, fairly dull. Skip Guarda, following signs to Aveiro. Soon the Coimbra road winds you through the beautiful Serra da Estrela mountains, forests, and villages that make it clear you're no longer in Spain. The many ambulances serve to remind you that Portugal is one of Europe's more dangerous countries to drive in. Your best offense is a good defense.

Expect no hassles at the border. The tourist office (on the right, open 9:00-19:00) is next to a decent bank.

Don't even think of driving into old Coimbra. You'll wonder why locals do. Park the car near the river and leave it. Leave absolutely nothing inside. As you enter town (along the river), you'll see Pensáo Jardim (Av. Navarro 65). You can turn right about 100 yards before it and park in the wildly rutted vacant lot.

By Bus and Train

Buses connect Salamanca and Ciudad Rodrigo with surprising efficiency in about an hour. But to reach Coimbra, unless you take the night train, you'll spend most of the day on the train or bus. There are two Coimbra train stations: A and B. Major trains all stop at B (big). From there, it's easy to catch a small train to the very central A station (take the A train). From the Coimbra bus station, turn right and prepare for a long, rotten, introductory walk.

Consider the city bus or, better, taxi to the town center at Largo da Portagem—but don't leave the bus station without the schedules to Nazaré and Batalha. If you arrive by train and are busing to Nazaré, avoid the long walk by asking at the Turismo for a travel agency that sells bus tickets. Get the train schedule to Lisbon, Nazaré and Óbidos to help your planning your arrival in Lisbon (read ahead). Train information: 27263 or 34998.

Ciudad Rodrigo

This rough-and-tumble old town of 16,000 people caps a hill overlooking the Río Agueda. Spend an hour wandering among the Renaissance mansions that line its streets and exploring its cathedral and Plaza Mayor. Have lunch or a snack at El Sanatorio (Plaza Mayor 14). The tapas are cheap, the crowd is local, and the walls are a Ciudad Rodrigo scrapbook, including some bullfighting that makes the three stooges look demure.

Ciudad Rodrigo's cathedral has some entertaining carving in the *coro* (choir) and some pretty racy work in its cloisters. Who said, "When you've seen one Gothic church, you've seen 'em all"?

The tourist information office is just inside the old wall, near the cathedral (tel. 923/46 05 61). The Plaza Mayor is a two-block walk from there.

Welcome to Portugal

The traveler's life changes when crossing into Portugal. The first thing you may notice is the change of time—if it's daylight savings you've gained an hour.

Also, the Spanish peseta gives way to the Portuguese escudo (confusingly indicated by a $ after the amount), which was 160 to the dollar in the summer of '93. Based on that rate, 100 escudos = about 65 cents. To convert escudos to dollars, cover the two zeros to the left of the $ mark and take two-thirds of what's left. So a meal costing

1000$ escudos is about 7 dollars, a 3000$ room about 20 dollars. Got it? Devise your own quick-'n'-easy conversion formula based on the current rate. Coins come in 1- to 200-escudo sizes, while bills range from 500 to 10,000. Learn the money—we'll be in Portugal for the next week.

Travelers checks cost a small fortune to cash (the average fee is about 12 dollars no matter how much you cash), so if this is what you're using be sure to shop around for the best commission/fee and try to cash in all your checks at one bank. You'll find automatic bill-changing machines everywhere. You can use them with bills from other countries as there is no fee.

Here's a reminder about hotel prices now that you're in Portugal:

very cheap	under $17	under 2,700$
cheap	$17-26	2,700-4,000$
inexpensive	$26-45	4,000-7,000$
moderate	$45-65	7,000-10,000$
expensive	over $65	over 10,000$

Occupying about one-fifth of the Iberian peninsula, at the extreme southwest corner of Europe, Portugal has always been off the beaten track. You'll find the pace of life is noticeably slower than Spain. Roads are rutted. Prices are cheaper. Parts of Lisbon feel almost Third World. The economy (one of the weakest in the EC) is based on fishing, cork, wine, and manufacturing.

The Portuguese language sounds like a blend of Spanish and French and is difficult to master quickly. In cities and along the Algarve you can usually find someone who speaks English. With my paltry Portuguese I communicate with bits of Spanish, French and sign language. My *Spanish & Portuguese Phrasebook* will help you hurdle the language barrier. A few useful words are *bom dia* (hello), *obrigado(a)* (thank you) and *adeus* (goodbye).

Coimbra

Don't be fooled by the ugly suburbs and monotonous concrete apartment buildings that surround the town. Portugal's most important city for 200 years, Coimbra (pronounced KWEEM-bra) remains second only to Lisbon culturally and historically. It was the center of Portugal while the Moors still controlled Lisbon. Only as Portugal's maritime fortunes rose was Coimbra surpassed by the ports of Lisbon and Porto. Today Coimbra is Portugal's third-largest city (pop. 100,000) with its oldest and most prestigious university (founded 1307) and a great Arab-flavored old quarter, complete with little kids who repeatedly ask, "What time is it now?"

Coimbra is a mini-Lisbon—everything good about urban Portugal without the intensity of a big city. I couldn't design a more enjoyable city for a visit. There's a small-town feeling in the winding streets set on the side of the hill. The high point is the old university. From there, little lanes meander down like a Moroccan medina to Rua de Ferreira Borges, the main business and shopping street, and the Mondego River. The crowded, intense Old Quarter of town is the triangle between the river and the Rua de Ferreira Borges. When school is in session, Coimbra bustles. During school holidays, it's sleepier.

From the Largo da Portagem (main square), everything is within an easy walk. The Old Quarter spreads out like an amphitheater—time-worn houses, shops, and stairways, all leading up to the university. The best views are looking up from the south end of Santa Clara Bridge, and looking down from the balcony of the university.

The most direct route up the hill is to follow Rua de Ferreira Borges away from the Largo da Portagem, then turn right under a twelfth-century arch (the marketplace is down the stairs to your left) and go up the steep alley called Rua de Quebra Costas—"Street of Broken Ribs." Two little squares later, you'll hit the fortresslike old cathedral. Beyond that is the university.

The tourist office (Largo da Portagem, tel. 039/23886, open Monday-Friday 9:00-19:00, Saturday and Sunday 9:00-12:30, 14:00-17:30, no information on trains or buses) and plenty of good budget rooms are along the river, three blocks from the train station. Navigate using the more detailed backside of the tourist office city map. Beware of banks charging outrageous commissions to cash traveler's checks. Telephone code: 039.

Coimbra

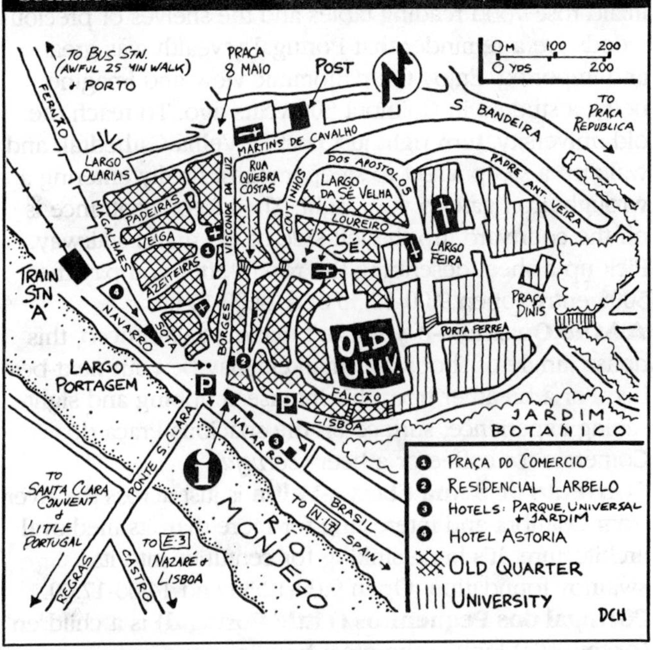

Sightseeing Highlights—Coimbra

Se Velha (Old Cathedral)—This dinky Romanesque church is built like a bulky but compact fortress, complete with crenellations. There's an interesting flamboyant Gothic altarpiece and a peaceful early Gothic cloister (open 9:00-12:30 and 14:00-17:00).

▲Old University—Coimbra's 700-year-old university was modeled after the Bologna university (Europe's first, A.D.. 1139). It's a stately, three-winged former royal palace (from when Coimbra was capital), beautifully situated overlooking the city. At first, law, medicine, grammar, and logic were taught. Then, with Portugal's seafaring orientation, astronomy and geometry were added. Three sections are open to you and worthwhile: the Sala dos Capelos, where degrees were given (check out the portraits of Portuguese kings and the nearby catwalk); the Manueline-style chapel (with its lavish organ loft); and the rich library (with thousands of old books and historical documents surrounded by gilded ceilings and baroque halls). The inlaid rosewood reading tables and the shelves of precious woods are a reminder that Portugal's wealth was great, and imported. Enjoy the panoramic view and imagine being a student in Coimbra 500 years ago. To reach the old university, turn right just past Se Velha Cathedral, and walk up a steep street to steeper steps, finally entering a wrought iron gate to your right. The visitor's entrance is off the courtyard, up the left side of the grand stairway. Pick up a sheet describing the rooms after you pay the 500$ entry (open 9:00-12:30 and 14:00-19:00).

▲▲Old Quarter—If you can't make it to Morocco, this dense jungle of shops and markets may be your next-best bet. For a breather from this intense shopping and sightseeing experience, surface on the spacious Praça do Comércio for coffee or a beer (*cerveja*).

Convento de Santa Clara-a-Velha is just across the river from Coimbra and interesting for more than its medieval architecture. It's been sinking for centuries into its swampy foundation. Open 9:00-12:30 and 14:00-17:00.

Portugal dos Pequenitos (Little Portugal) is a children's (or tourist's) look at the great buildings and monuments of Portugal, in miniature, scattered through the park. A good introduction to the country for those just entering and wishing they had more time (9:00-19:00 daily, 350$).

Conimbriga Roman Ruins—Not much of this Roman city has survived the ravages of time and barbarians. Still, there are some good floor mosaics and a museum—a few miles south of Coimbra on the Lisbon road, turn left to Condeixa; buses run to Condeixa, leaving about a mile walk; the Turismo has the schedule—open 9:00-13:00 and 14:00-20:00; museum closed Monday.

Sleeping and Eating in Coimbra—telephone code: 039, postal code 3000.

The driver's easiest bet is to choose one of the places that line the riverside Avenida E. Navarro at the base of town within a block or two of Santa Clara Bridge (the road from Spain) and within four blocks of the train station. They have noisy front rooms, so choose the rear or consider one of my recommendations off the river, in the city center. Warning: almost no one speaks English. Try broken Spanish, French or sign language.

The **Pensão Residencial Jardim** at 65 Av. Navarro is excellent. It's an elegant old family-run place bursting with nice touches that have been around since the turn of the century. It has giant, well-appointed, well-lit rooms and a TV lounge (inexpensive, tel. 25204). Just down the street at #47, just as old, and cheaper, but without the charm and personal touch, is the **Residencial Universal** (cheap, tel. 22444). Next on the strip at #37 is **Hotel Avenida** (moderate, tel. 22156) . . . more normal but less fun. And for those who want the thrill of spending only around $80 and staying in the city's finest, you can go stuffy at the riverside and central-as-can-be **Hotel Astoria** (expensive, Av. Navarro 21, tel. 22055, fax. 22 057). Behind the Astoria is the infinitely friendlier and cheaper **Pensão Vitoria**, basically a restaurant with twelve rooms tucked away upstairs. If you're on a budget, this is a good bet (cheap, with a shower, Rua da Sota 3, tel. 24049).

On the Largo da Portagem, in front of the bridge is **Residencial Larbelo** (inexpensive, Largo da Portagem 33, tel. 29092), which mixes frumpiness and well-worn elegance beautifully. The royal staircase makes you almost glad there's no elevator.

Rivoli Pensão offers the best location, three blocks off the river on the lovable **Praça do Comércio** (cheap, Praça do Comércio 27, tel. 25550). It's a bit eccentric but a fine value.

Adventurous softies will enjoy **Hospedaria Simões**, buried in the exotic heart of the cobbled hillside, just below the old cathedral. Run by the friendly Simões family, it offers bright, clean rooms but almost no windows (cheap, all with shower, Rua Fernandes Tomas 69, tel. 34638).

The **youth hostel**, **Pousada de Juventude** (Rua Antonio Henriques Seco 14, tel. 22955, closed from 12:00-18:00), on the other side of town in the student area past the Praça da Republica, is friendly, clean, well-run, and comfortable, but no cheaper than a simple pensão.

This is a town filled with fun and cheap eateries. Wander the old town between the river and the Praça do Comércio. I found great deals in the medina on ruas Dirieta and Azeiteiras. If chicken sounds good, **Churrasquería do Mondego** (Rua do Sargento Mor 27, near Largoda Portagem) serves a cheap soup/chicken/mousse/wine meal in a fun assembly-line diner kind of way. For a decent meal on a great square, eat at **Restaurant Praça Velha** (on Praça do Comércio). There are a few local-style cafés near the old cathedral. For a classy splurge in one of these, eat at **Restaurant Trovador** (across from the old cathedral).

DAY 6

COIMBRA, BATALHA, AND FATIMA TO NAZARÉ

Spend the morning browsing around Portugal's easiest-to-enjoy city, then travel to the huge Gothic monastery at Batalha. After rubbing elbows with the pilgrims at Fatima, set up in Nazaré, your beach-town headquarters on the Atlantic.

Suggested Schedule—By Car

8:00	Breakfast in hotel or with busy locals in a bar on Rua de Ferreira Borges.
8:30	Enjoy a shady morning in the Old Quarter alleys and shops. (Buy a picnic lunch.) Or tour Little Portugal or the Conimbriga Roman Ruins.
11:30	Drive to Batalha.
13:00	Picnic, then tour Batalha Church (Monastery of Santa Maria).
16:00	Side trip to pilgrimage site of Fatima, then drive into Nazaré.
18:00	Drive into Nazaré and set up.

The Route: Coimbra to Batalha to Nazaré (60 miles)
You'll cross Santa Clara Bridge and follow signs to Lisbon and Leiria. You'll see Batalha, proud and ornate, on the left of the highway, in 90 minutes. From Batalha, it's a pleasant drive down N356, then N242 into Nazaré.

By Bus and Train
Head directly to Nazaré, set up, and visit Batalha tomorrow by bus from Nazaré. A few direct buses connect Coimbra with Nazaré daily in about 2.5 hours. The train goes five times a day from Coimbra to Nazaré's Velado station (3.5 hours) with a change in Figueira da Foz. Velado station is the nearest train station to Nazaré (3 miles away) with semi-regular bus connections and reasonable taxis (information tel. 51172). If you want to see

Nazaré Region

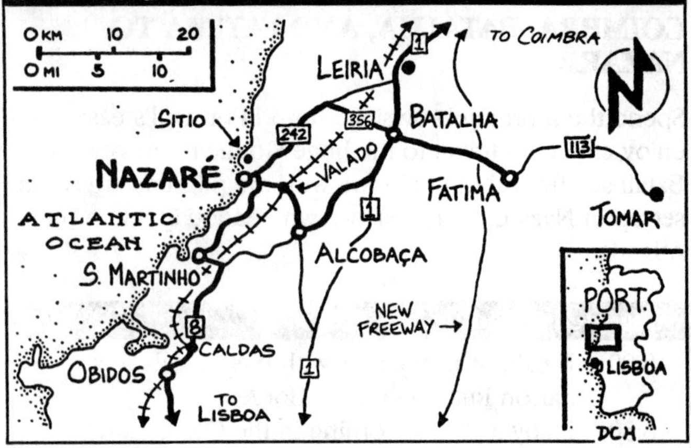

Fatima on a tight schedule, rent a car in Nazaré for the day and see Batalha as well. Bus transport to Fatima takes too long. Turn right out of Nazaré's bus station and right on the ocean-front street to reach my hotel listings.

Sightseeing Highlights

▲▲Batalha: The Monastery of Santa María—This is considered Portugal's greatest architectural achievement and a symbol of its national pride. Batalha (which means "battle") was begun in 1388 to thank God for a Portuguese victory that kept it free from Spanish rule. The greatness of Portugal's Age of Discovery shines brightly in the royal cloisters, which combine the simplicity of Gothic with the elaborate decoration of the fancier Manueline style, and in the chapter house with its frighteningly broad vaults. The heavy ceiling was considered so dangerous to build (it collapsed twice) that only prisoners condemned to death were allowed to work on it. Today it's considered stable enough for foreigners to visit and to be the home of the Portuguese tomb of the unknown soldier. Also visit the Founder's Chapel to see its many royal tombs, including Henry the Navigator's (Henry's the one wearing a church on his head). The Batalha abbey is great, but nothing else at this stop is (open 9:00-18:00 daily, Turismo tel. 049/96180).

▲▲**Fatima**—On May 13, 1917, the Virgin Mary, "a lady brighter than the sun," visited three young shepherds and told them peace was needed. World War I raged on, so on the 13th of each of the next five months, Mary dropped in again to call for peace. On the 13th of October, 70,000 witnessed the parting of dark storm clouds as the sun wrote "God's fiery signature" across the sky. Now, on the 13th of each month, thousands of pilgrims gather at the huge neoclassical basilica of Fatima (evening torchlit parades on the 12th and 13th). In 1930, the Vatican recognized Fatima as legit and on the fiftieth anniversary, 1.5 million pilgrims, including the Pope, gathered here. Fatima welcomes guests. If you are driving, Fatima is an easy and interesting (for some) side trip (though not so easy around the 13th) just twelve miles east of Batalha. The impressive Basilica do Rosário stands in front of a mammoth square lined with parks. Surrounding the square are hotels, restaurants, and tacky souvenir stands. Visitors may want to check out the Museo de Cera de Fatima, a wax museum story of Fatima, and the Museu-Vivo Aparicões for a high-tech sound and light show that re-creates of the apparition (both open daily 9:00-19:00, modest dress for the basilica, Turismo tel. 049/531139).

Nazaré

See Day 7

DAY 7

BEACH DAY IN NAZARÉ, ALCOBAÇA SIDE TRIP

After all the traveling you've done, it's time for an easy day and some sun in the fun. Between two nights in your beach town, take a 30-mile triangular side trip, spend the afternoon soaking up the sun, and enjoy an evening of fresh shrimp and *vinho verde* in colorful, fishy Nazaré. Watch the boats come in as the shells pile up and the sun sets.

Suggested Schedule

By Car

8:00	Breakfast at hotel.
8:30	Drive through countryside, visiting the wine museum, Alcobaça (town and monastery), and São Martinho do Porto.
13:00	Lunch back in Nazaré, ride the funicular up to Sitio, free time on beaches.
19:00	Seafood dinner.

By Bus

If you leave Nazaré today it will be by bus. Good daytrip destinations are Alcobaça, Batalha, and Óbidos. Get schedule information at Nazaré's bus station: 6-8 buses per day make the 1-hour run to Batalha, 12 buses per day connect Nazaré and Alcobaça in 30 minutes, and 6 per day make the 1-hour run to Óbidos. Batalha and Alcobaça are linked by a 1-hour bus trip 6-8 times per day—if you choose to do both, see Batalha first.

▲▲Nazaré

Nazaré doesn't have any blockbuster sights. The colorful fish market (Mercado de Peixe, 6:00-14:00) near the beach on the south edge of town, the beach, and the funicular ride (60$) up to Sitio for some shopping and a great coastal view, along with the "sightseeing" my taste buds did, are the bright lights of my lazy Nazaré memories.

Plan for some beach time here. Ask at the tourist office about bullfights in the Sitio (most summer weekends) and folk-dancing at the casino (two nights a week in the summer). Sharing a bottle of *vinho verde*, a new wine specialty of north Portugal, on the beach at sundown is a good way to wrap up the day.

In the summer, it seems that most of this famous town's 10,000 inhabitants are in the tourist trade. Nazaré is a hit with the Portuguese as well as international tour groups and masses of day-trippers who come up from Lisbon to see traditionally clad fishermen mend traditional nets to catch traditional fish. The beach promenade is a congested tangle of oily sunbathers, hustlers, plastic souvenirs, dogs engaged in public displays of affection, overpriced restaurants, and, until they built the new harbor, romantic fishing boats. Off-season, however, Nazaré is almost empty of tourists—inexpensive, colorful, and relaxed.

Any time of year, even with its crowds, almost even in August, Nazaré is a fun stop offering a surprisingly good look at old Portugal. Somehow the traditions survive and the locals are able to go about their black-shawl ways, ignoring the tourists. Wander the back streets for a fine look at Portuguese family-in-the-street life. Your best home base is the town center directly below the Sitio.

Nazaré faces its long beach, stretching from the new harbor north to Sitio, the hill-capping old town. The Sitio, which feels like a totally separate village, sits relatively quiet atop its cliff, and is reached by a frequent funicular. Go up at least for the spectacular view, but there are some good eateries and shops, too. And Sitio stages bullfights (Portuguese style—they don't kill the bull) on Saturday evenings in the summer (22:00, 1,000-3,000$ tickets from the kiosk in Pr. Souza Oliveiro).

The indifferent tourist office is on the Avenida da República, the main beach front street (open daily 10:00-22:00, shorter hours off-season, tel. 56 11 94). Telephone code: 062.

Sleeping and Eating in Nazaré, telephone code: 062, postal code 2450.

You should have no problem finding a room except in August, when the crowds, temperatures, and prices are all at their highest. You'll find plenty of hustlers meeting each bus and along the promenade. I've never arrived in town without a welcome committee inviting me to sleep in their place. There are lots of *quartos* (rooms in private homes) and cheap, dingy pensions. I stay at the end of town near the high cliffs, as close to the water as possible. Prices are higher, but it's worthwhile. Prices listed are for summer, July through mid-October; they fall by around 50 percent off-season. I've never seen an elevator in Nazaré.

Residencial Cubata (moderate, Avenida da República 6, tel. 062/56 17 06) is a friendly place on the waterfront above the Bingo sign on the north (high cliffs) end; my favorite waterfront hotel value.

Ribamir Hotel Restaurant (expensive, Praça Sousa Oliveira 67-A, tel. 062/551158) has a prime location on the waterfront, with an Old World, classy, well-worn, musty, hotelesque atmosphere, including dark wood and four-poster beds. Look for the yellow awnings.

Mar Bravo Pensão is on the corner where the main square meets the waterfront next to Ribamir. Though it seems more money-grubbing and has less character, it's modern, bright, and fresh, with a good restaurant downstairs and a new face-lift (expensive, Praça Sousa Oliviera 67-A, tel. 062/551180).

Restaurante "O Navegante" has three doubles, one very small and cheap, and a shower down the hall; it's about three blocks inland, and usually someone around speaks some English (inexpensive, turn right just before the Tourist office and walk up about four blocks—it's at Rua Adrião Batalha 89-A, tel. 55 18 93). The cheapest option always is to find a private home renting out a room. Just ask for "quartos." They're everywhere. The friendly owners of Casa dos Frango's chicken deli have a few well-located quartos near the water on the Praca Dr Manual Arriaga.

Nazaré is a fishing town, so don't order *hamburguesas.* Fresh seafood is great all over town, more expensive (but affordable) along the waterfront, cheap in holes-in-walls farther inland. I like the places near the funicular station. Consider dining up in Sitio with a panoramic view. Try the local drinks—Amendoa Amarga (like amaretto) and Licor Beirão. Chicken addicts can try Casa dos Frango's roasted chickens-to-go (look under hotels for location) and picnic-gatherers should head for the covered mercado across from the bus station.

Sleeping in São Martinho do Porto, near Nazaré, telephone code: 062, postal code: 2465.
To avoid some of the crowds and enjoy about the warmest water on Portugal's west coast with a good beach arcing around a nearly landlocked (and fairly polluted) saltwater lake, stay in a small village eight miles south—São Martinho do Porto (pronounced "sow marteen yo"). Regular bus and train service from Nazaré make this a convenient alternative for public transport users as well. Turismo is right on the beach promenade in the town center (tel. 062/98 91 10, open 9:00-19:00 daily in summer). The grand old **Hotel Parque** (moderate, closed off-season, is a few blocks inland near the post office on Avenida Marchal Carmona, tel. 989505), with its clay tennis courts, stucco ceilings and a peaceful park, is a terrific semi-splurge. **Pensão Americana** (inexpensive-moderate rooms with showers and English-speaking owners, Rua D. José Saldanha, tel. 062/98 91 70) is a block from the beach. Plenty of quartos rent doubles for around 3,000$ in the summer, through the Turismo. Wander up and into San Martinho's old town for the best food prices and the town's covered mercado.

There's a fine youth hostel, **Pousada de Juventude**, on a hill about 6 kilometers away, above the village of Alfeizerão (on the main road, just before the São Martinho turnoff, tel. 99 95 06).

Alcobaça Side Trip
Leaving Nazaré, you'll pass women wearing the traditional seven petticoats (trust me) as they do laundry at the edge

of town on the road to Alcobaça (follow signs, then right at unmarked intersection). Within a few minutes you'll be surrounded by eucalyptus groves in a world that smells like a coughdrop. Then you land in Alcobaça (signs to "monuments"), famous for its church, the biggest in Portugal and one of the most interesting. Turismo is across the square from the church (tel. 062/42377).

Sightseeing Highlights

▲▲Alcobaça's Cistercian Mosteiro de Santa María—This abbey is the best Gothic building in Portugal, a clean and bright break from the heavier Iberian norm. Don't miss the fourteenth-century sarcophagi of Portugal's most romantic and tragic couple, Dom Pedro and Dona Inês de Castro. They rest feet-to-feet in each transept, so that on Judgment Day they'll rise and immediately see each other again. Pedro, heir to the Portuguese throne, was in love with the Spanish aristocrat, Inês. Concerned about Spanish influence, Pedro's father, Alfonso V, forbade their marriage. You guessed it—they were married secretly. Alfonso, in the interest of Portuguese independence, had Inês murdered. When Pedro became king (1357) he personally ripped out and ate the hearts of the murderers and, even more interestingly, he had Inês's rotten corpse exhumed, crowned it, and made the entire royal court kiss what was left of her hand. Now that's *amore.* (The carvings on the tomb are just as special.)

Pay the 200$ admission (buy the English leaflet) to tour the abbey cloister with the interesting kings' room (Sala dos Reis, statues of most of Portugal's kings) and the king-size kitchen with its huge chimney, marble table, and the impressive plumbing of a rerouted little river (open 9:00-19:00).

▲Alcobaça's Mercado Municipal (daily 9:00-13:00, closed Sunday, best on Mondays) will always shine brightly in my memory. It houses the Old World happily under its huge steel and glass dome. Inside, black-clad, dried-apple-faced women choose fish, chicks, birds, and rabbits from their respective death rows. You'll also find figs, melons, bushels of grain, and nuts—it's a caveman's Safeway. Buying a picnic is a perfect excuse to drop in.

▲▲Museu Nacional do Vinho—A half-mile outside town (on the road to Batalha and Leiria, right-hand side) you'll find the local cooperative winery, which runs the National Museum of Wine, a fascinating look at the wine of Portugal, (9:00-12:00 and 14:00-17:00, closed Saturday and Sunday; for safety, park inside gate). The museum teaches you everything you never wanted to know about Portuguese wine, in a series of rooms that used to be fermenting vats. With some luck you can get a tour, much more hands-on than French winery tours, through the actual winery. You'll see mountains of centrifuged, strained, and drained grapes—all well on the road to wine. Ask if you can climb to the top of one of twenty half-buried, white, 80,000-gallon tanks, all busy fermenting. Look out. I stuck my head into the manhole-sized top vent, and just as I focused on the rich, bubbling grape stew, I was walloped silly by a wine-vapor punch.

Return via the tiny fishing village of São Martinho do Porto (road to Caldas from Alcobaça's church). Back in Nazaré, you'll be greeted by the energetic applause of the forever surf and big plates of smiling steamed shrimp.

DAY 8

NAZARÉ, ÓBIDOS, AND LISBON

Today you'll travel just 60 miles in distance but centuries in time, leaving the traditional beach village to spend a few hours in Portugal's cutest walled city, and then driving into modern Lisbon, where you'll set up for three nights.

Suggested Schedule—By Car

9:00	Leave Nazaré.
10:00	Explore Óbidos.
12:00	Drive into Lisbon, set up, visit tourist office.
14:00	Stroll Avenida de Liberdade, explore downtown Rossio and Baixa center, lunch and shop. Joy-ride on trolley #28.
18:00	Evening and dinner at Feira Popular (May-September) or in the Alfama.

Note: Bullfights are at 22:00 on many Thursdays and Sundays near Feira Popular. Museums (including Gulbenkian, Pena Palace at Sintra, and the Belem sights) are closed on Mondays.

The Route: Nazaré to Óbidos to Lisbon (60 miles)
Drivers will follow N242 south from Nazaré, passing São Martinho, and catching scenic N8 farther south to Óbidos. Don't even think about driving in tiny, cobbled Óbidos. Ample tourist parking is provided outside town. From Óbidos, take the no-nonsense direct route—N115, N1, and E3 into Lisbon, or consider leaving your car in Óbidos and taking the cheap stress-free train into the heart of Lisbon.

Driving in Lisbon is big-city crazy. A series of boulevards take you into the center. Navigate by following signs to Centro, Avenida da Republica, Pr. Marques de Pombal, Avenida da Liberdade, Pr. Restauradores, Rossio, and Pr. do Comércio. Consider hiring a taxi (cheap) to lead you to your hotel.

There's an easy and safe pay lot underground at Pr. Restauradores (under the obelisk). Cheap at first, it gets more expensive by the hour, up to 3,500$ per day. It's next to the Turismo, within a five-minute walk of most of my hotel listings. Ask at your hotel about safe parking in a city whose parking lots glitter with the crumbled remains of wing windows.

By Bus and Train

While several daily bus or train trips connect Nazaré and Obidos in less than an hour, (you choose—the bus gets you closer to the center), and there's good direct train service to Lisbon from Óbidos, it's best to do Óbidos as a bus day-trip from Nazaré rather then enroute to Lisbon. The Óbidos bus stop and train station are not equipped to handle left luggage—and the train station is a hilly 10-minute walk from the town center (it's downhill from the station; ask "centro?"). Either way, arrive in Lisbon by train—several direct trips run from Nazaré and Obidos into Lisbon's very central Rossio station—where you'll be a short walk from most of my listed hotels.

Óbidos

This medieval walled town was Portugal's "wedding city"—the perfect gift for kings whose queens had everything. (Beats a toaster.) Today it's preserved in its entirety as a national monument, surviving on tourism. Óbidos is crowded all summer, especially in August. Filter out the tourists; view it as you would a beautiful painted tile. It's worth a quick visit.

Postcard perfect, the town sits atop a hill, its 40-foot-high wall corraling a bouquet of narrow lanes and flower-bedecked, whitewashed houses. Óbidos is ideal for photographers who want to make Portugal look prettier than it is. Walk around the wall, peek into the castle (now an overly-impressed-with-itself pousada, tel. 062/95 91 05, fax 959 148), lose yourself for a while in this lived-in open-air museum of medieval city nonplanning. Wander the back lanes, study the solid centuries-old houses. There's a small museum, an interesting Renaissance church with lovely azulejo walls inside, and, outside the walls, an aqueduct, a windmill, and a market.

Óbidos is tough on the budget. Pick up a picnic at the grocery store just inside the main gate or from the tiny market just outside. If you spend the night, you'll enjoy the town without tourists. Two good values in this sterilized and overpriced touristic toy of a town are **Albergasia Rainha Santa Isabel** (moderate, on the town's main one-lane drag, Rua Direita, tel. 959115) and **Casa do Poco** (moderate, in the old center near the castle, tel. 95 93 58). For less expensive intimacy, ask around for quartos (private rooms). In the spirit of profit maximization, the Óbidos tourist office (9:30 to 19:00, tel. 95 92 31) doesn't give out quartos information.

Lisbon
See Day 9.

DAY 9

LISBON

Plunge into Lisbon's urban jungle, tasting its salty sailors' quarter, exploring its hill-capping castle, enjoying some world-class art, and eating, sipping, and browsing your way through its colorful shopping districts. Wrap up the day atmospherically with seafood and folk music.

Suggested Schedule

8:00	Breakfast.
9:00	Tour castle São Jorge. Coffee break at café next to Miradour de Santa Luzia, then descend by the long stairway into the Alfama. Explore. Meander.
12:00	Lunch in Alfama or at O Policia near museum.
14:00	Tour Gulbenkian Art Museum.
16:00	Taxi to Chiado district, shop along Rua Garrett, have coffee at A Brasiliera, explore Baírro Alto, view the city from San Pedro Terrace. Ride the funicular back downtown.
18:30	Relax at hotel.
20:00	Taxi to Cervejaría da Trinidade for dinner or go to a dinner/fado show in the Baírro Alto neighborhood.

Lisbon

Lisbon is a wonderful mix of now and then. Old wooden trolleys shiver up and down its hills, bird-stained statues mark grand squares, taxis rattle and screech through cobbled lanes, and well-worn people sip coffee in art nouveau cafés.

Present-day Lisbon is explained by its past. While its history goes back to the Romans and the Moors, the glory days were the fifteenth and sixteenth centuries when explorers like Vasco da Gama opened new trade routes around Africa to India, making Lisbon one of Europe's richest cities. The economic boom brought the flamboyant art boom called the Manueline period, named after King

Manuel the Fortunate. Later, in the early eighteenth century, the riches (gold and diamonds) of Brazil (one of Portugal's colonies) made Lisbon even wealthier.

Then, on All Saints Day in 1755, while most of the population was in church, the city was hit by a tremendous earthquake, felt all the way to Ireland. Lisbon was dead center. Two-thirds of the city was leveled; fires, started by the many church candles, raged; and a huge tidal wave blasted the waterfront. Forty thousand of Lisbon's 270,000 people were killed.

But Lisbon was rebuilt, in a progressive grid plan with broad boulevards and square squares, under the energetic and eventually dictatorial leadership of the Marquis Pombal. The charm of pre-earthquake Lisbon survives only in Belem, the Alfama, and the Baírro Alto district.

In more recent years, Portugal lost its vast empire, the last bits let go with the 1974 revolution that delivered her from the right-wing Salazar dictatorship. Emigrants from such former colonies as Mozambique and Angola have added diversity and flavor to the city, making it more likely that you'll hear African music than fado these days.

In 1988, another disaster struck as a huge fire destroyed much of the Chiado's most elegant shopping district. But Lisbon's heritage survives. The city seems better-organized, cleaner, and more prosperous and people-friendly now than in the 1980s. Barely elegant outdoor cafés, exciting art, bustling bookstores, entertaining museums (closed on Mondays), the saltiest sailors' quarter in Europe, and much more, all at bargain basement prices, make Lisbon a world-class city.

Lisbon Orientation

Lisbon is easy. The city center is a series of parks, boulevards, and squares bunny-hopping between two hills down to the waterfront. The center is Rossio Square, with plenty of buses, subways, and cheap taxis leaving in all directions. Between the Rossio and the harbor is the flat lower city, the Baixa (pronounced bai-shah), with its checkerboard street plan, elegant architecture, bustling shops, and many cafés. Most of Lisbon's prime attractions are within walking distance of the Rossio.

Lisbon

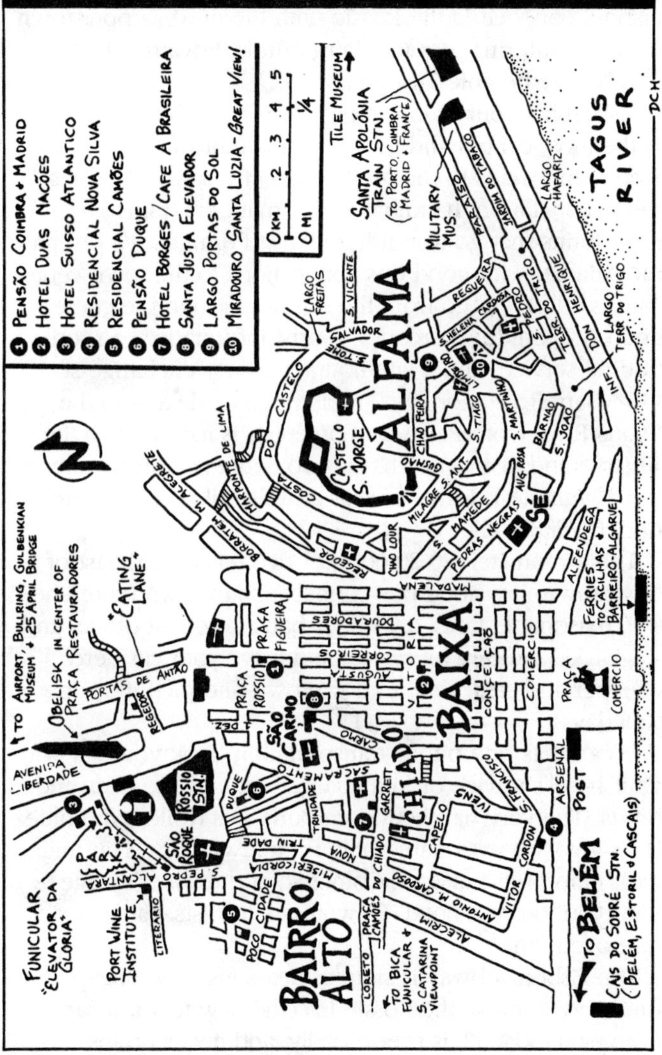

On a hill to the west of the Rossio is the old and noble shopping district of the Chiado. Above that is Lisbon's "Latin Quarter," the Baírro Alto (upper quarter) with dark bars, hidden restaurants, and weepy fado places.

East of the Rossio is another hill, blanketed by the medieval Alfama quarter and capped by Castelo São Jorge.

Avenida Liberdade is the tree-lined "Champs Elysées" of Lisbon, connecting the Rossio with the newer upper town (airport, bull ring, popular fairgrounds, Edward VII Park, and breezy botanical gardens).

Lisbon has four train stations (see map). Rossio station is the most central and handles most trains from Óbidos, Sintra, and trains to the west and north. Santa Apolonia is the major station, handling all international trains and most trains that go to north and east Portugal. It's just past the Alfama, with good bus connections to the town center (buses #9 or #46 go from the station through the center and up Avenida Liberdade), tourist information, a room-finding service, and a late-hours currency exchange service. Barreiro station, a 30-minute ferry ride across the Tagus River from Praça do Comércio, is for trains to the Algarve and points south. Caís do Sodre station handles the 30-minute rides to Cascais and Estoril. Train information: 01/888 4025.

The airport (tel. 80 20 60), just five miles northeast of downtown, has good bus connections to town (take line 90), reasonable taxis, a 24-hour bank, a tourist office, and a guarded parking lot (you could leave your car here cheaper and safer than in downtown and pick it up in two days).

Lisbon has fine public transportation. Park your car with your hotel's advice or in a guarded lot and use taxis and buses. The very handy underground lots (follow the blue "P" signs) are reasonable only for a few hours. You might park here or at Praça do Comércio at the water's edge until you locate a hotel. Downtown, tourists' cars are not safe overnight.

The Lisbon subway is simple, clean, fast, and cheap, but runs only north of the Rossio into the new town. It runs from 6:00 to 24:00, is user-friendly, and needs no instructions. The big letter "M" marks metro stops. The bus system is very extensive and worth the time it takes to figure out.

For more fun and practical public transport, use the trolley system, the funicular, and the Eiffel-esque elevator (cheap, buy tickets at the door, going every few minutes) to connect the lower and upper towns. Lisbon taxis are cheap, abundant, and use their meters.

The main tourist information office at the lower end of Avenida Liberdade in the Palacio da Foz at Praça dos Restauradores, three blocks north of Rossio (daily 9:00-20:00, tel. 346-3643), gives out information with a snarl. Pick up a city map and their brochure on current events. There are also offices in the Apolonia train station and at the airport. The best periodical entertainment guide is *Se7e*, available at newsstands. There's a very handy train information office on the ground floor of the Rossio station.

Banks, the post office, airlines, and travel agents line the Avenida Liberdade. American Express is in the Top Tours office at Ave. Duque de Loule 108, tel. 315 5877, open weekdays 9:00-13:00 and 14:30-18:30. The telephone center on Rossio Square is open daily until 23:00. Telephone code: 01.

Sightseeing Highlights—Lisbon

▲▲Rossio and Baixa—When the earthquake of 1755 was over, Pombal rebuilt the town center on a logical grid plan with uniform five-story buildings. In the last few years several streets have been turned into charming pedestrian zones, making this area more enjoyable than ever. The mosaicked Rua Augusta is every bit as delightful as Barcelona's Ramblas for strolling. Lisbon's Sè, or cathedral, just a few blocks east of Praça do Comércio, is not much on the inside, but its fortresslike exterior is a textbook example of a stark and powerful Romanesque fortress of God. Started in 1150, its crenellated towers made a powerful statement after Lisbon was reconquered from the Moors.

▲Ride a trolley—Lisbon's vintage trolleys, most from the 1920s, shake and shiver all over town, somehow safely weaving within inches of parked cars, climbing steep hills, and offering sightseers breezy wide-open-window views of the city. Line 28 from Graça to Prazeres offers a great Lisbon joy-ride. (Rice-a-roni!) Pick it up at Rua da Conceicào in Baixa. It goes through the Chiado to Estrela (Basilica and Park) and past the Alfama to Santa Clara near the flea market. Just pay the conductor as you board.

▲▲The Bairro Alto and Chiado Districts—The colorful upper city is reached by the funicular (Elevator da Gloria) and the (Santa Justa) elevator, both funky sights in themselves (140$ each). From the top of the funicular, enjoy the city view from the San Pedro Park belvedere. The Port Wine Institute is across the street and the São Roque Church is around the corner on Largo Trinidade Coelho.

São Roque looks like just another church, but wander slowly under its flat painted ceiling and notice the rich side chapels. The highlight is the Chapel of St. John the Baptist (left of altar) that looks like it came right out of the Vatican. It did. Made at the Vatican out of the most precious materials, it was the site of one papal mass; then it was taken down and shipped to Lisbon—probably the most costly chapel per square inch ever constructed. Notice the beautiful mosaic floor and the three paintings that are actually intricate mosaics, a Vatican specialty.

Continue into the Chiado down Rua da Misercordia (check out the chic Centro Commercial Espaco at #20) to Praça Luis de Camões. A left will take you onto a pleasant square (with the A Brasiliera café) to the classy Rua Garett. Another left (on Sacramento) takes you to another pleasant square with the ruins of the Convento do Carmo (peek in to see the elegant, earthquake-ruined, Gothic arches). From there, the elevator literally takes you downtown. Enjoy the city view while you wait.

▲▲▲Alfama—Europe's most colorful sailors' quarter goes way back to Visigothic days. It was a rich district during the Arabic period and finally the home of Lisbon's fisherfolk (and of the poet who wrote "our lips meet easily high across the narrow street"). One of the few areas to survive the 1755 earthquake, the Alfama is a cobbled playground of Old World color. A visit is best during the busy midmorning market time or in the late afternoon/early evening when the streets teem with locals.

Wander deep. This urban jungle's roads are squeezed into tangled and confusing alleys; bent houses comfort each other in their romantic shabbiness; and the air drips with laundry and the smell of clams and raw fish. Get lost. Poke aimlessly, sample ample grapes, avoid rabid-looking dogs, peek through windows. Don't miss Rua de São Pedro, the liveliest street around.

Electric streetcars #10, #11, and #26 go to the Alfama. On Tuesdays and Saturdays, the Feira da Ladra flea market rages on the nearby Campo de Santa Clara (bus #9 or #46, trolley #28). To start or finish your Alfama adventure at the top: use the Beco Santa Helena, a stairway that connects the maze with the Largo das Portas do Sol and the Miradouro de Santa Luzia view point. Probably the most scenic cup of coffee in town is enjoyed from the Cerca Moura bar/café (Largo das Portas do Sol 4, top of the stairs).

▲Castelo São Jorge—The city castle, with a history going back to Roman days, caps the highest hill above the Alfama and offers a pleasant garden and Lisbon's top view point. Use this perch to orient yourself. Open daily until sunset.

▲Fado—Mournfully beautiful, haunting ballads about lost sailors, broken hearts, and sad romance are one of Lisbon's favorite late-night tourist traps. Be careful, this is one of those cultural clichés that all too often become rip-offs. The Alfama has many touristy fado bars, but the Baírro Alto is your best bet. Things don't start until 22:00 and then take an hour or two to warm up. A fado performance isn't cheap (expect a 2,000\$-3,000\$ cover), and many fado joints require dinner. Ask at your hotel for advice.

▲▲Gulbenkian Museum—This is the best of Lisbon's 40 museums. Gulbenkian, an Armenian oil tycoon, gave his art collection (or "harem," as he called it) to Portugal in gratitude for the hospitable asylum granted him there during WW II. Now this great collection, spanning 2,000 years of art, is displayed in a classy and comfortable modern building. Ask for the excellent English text explaining the collection.

You'll stroll chronologically through the ages past the great Egyptian, Greek, and Middle Eastern sections. There are masterpieces by Rembrandt, Rubens, Renoir, Rodin, and artists whose names start with other letters. There are nice gardens and a good, cheap, air-conditioned cafeteria.

Take bus #15, #30, #31, #41, #46, or #56 from downtown or the Sete-Ríos metro line to the "Palhava" stop, or taxi from the Rossio. Open Tuesday, Thursday, Friday, and Sunday 10:00-17:00; Wednesday and Saturday 14:00-19:30 in summer; closed Monday. Tel. 793-5131. The recommended O Policia restaurant is nearby.

▲▲Museu Nacional de Arte Antigua—Lisbon's museum of ancient art is the country's best for Portuguese paintings from her glory days, the fifteenth and sixteenth centuries. You'll also find the great masters (Bosch, Jan van Eyck, and Raphael, to name just a few) and rich furniture, all in a grand palace (buses #27, #40, and #49 or tram #19; Rua das Janeles Verdes 9, open 10:00-13:00 and 14:00-17:00; closed Monday, tel. 396 6001).

▲Museu Nacional do Azulejo—This museum featuring tile is located in the Convento da Madre de Deus, a 10-minute ride on bus #13 from the S. Apolonia station. It's well worth a look for tile-lovers. Don't miss the Baroque church.

▲▲▲Bullfights—If you always felt sorry for the bull, this is Toro's Revenge; in a Portuguese bullfight, the matador is brutalized. In the Portuguese *tourada*, unlike the Spanish *corrida*, the bull is not killed. After an exciting equestrian prelude where the horseman (*cavaleiro*) skillfully plants barbs in the bull's back while trying to avoid the padded horns, a colorfully clad, eight-man team (suicide squad) enters the ring and lines up single file facing the bull. The leader prompts the bull to charge, then braces himself for a collision that can be heard all the way up in the cheap seats. As he hangs onto the bull's head, his buddies then pile on, trying to wrestle it to a standstill. Finally, one guy hangs on to *el toro*'s tail and "water-skis" behind him.

You're most likely to see a bullfight in Lisbon, Estoril, or on the Algarve. Get schedules in the tourist office; fights start late in the evening. In Lisbon, there are fights at Capo Pequeno Thursday nights only from July through September at 22:00, tickets from 2000$. Nearby arenas advertise fights on Sundays. The season lasts from Easter through October. Tickets are available at the door or from the kiosk across the square from the central tourist office.

▲▲**Feira Popular (The People's Fair)**—By all means spend an evening at Lisbon's Feira Popular, which bustles with Portuguese families at play. Pay the tiny entry fee, then enjoy rides, munchies, great people-watching, entertainment, music—basic Portuguese fun. Have dinner here among the chattering families, with endless food and wine paraded frantically in every direction. Food stalls dispense wine from the udders of porcelain cows. Fried ducks drip, barbecues spit, and dogs squirt the legs of chairs while, somehow, local lovers ignore everything but each other's eyes. (Nightly, May 1 to September 30 from 19:00 to midnight, Saturdays and Sundays 15:00 to midnight. Located on Avenida da República at the "Entre-Campos" metro stop.)

▲**Cristo Rei**—A huge statue of Christ (à la Rio de Janeiro) overlooks Lisbon from across the Tagus River. A lift takes you to the top, and the view is worth the effort. Boats leave from downtown constantly (buses connect every 15 minutes). A taxi will charge you round-trip, but it's exciting to get to ride over Lisbon's great bridge (open 10:00-18:00 daily).

▲**The 25th of April Bridge**, a mile long, is the third-longest suspension bridge in the world. Built in 1966, it was originally named for the dictator Salazar but renamed for the date of Portugal's revolution and freedom. Drivers will cross it as they head south.

Shopping

Lisbon is Europe's bargain basement. You'll find decaying but still-elegant department stores, teeming flea markets, classy specialty shops, and one of Europe's largest modern shopping centers. The Mercado Ribeira open-air market, next to the Caís do Sodre market, bustles every morning except Sunday—great for picnic stuff and local sweaters. Look for shoes, bags, and leather goods on Rua Garrett and Rua Carmo and gold and silver on the Rua do Ouro (Gold Street). And for the gleaming modern side of things, taxi to Amoreiras Shopping Center de Lisboa (Avda. da Duarte Pacheco; you can see its pink and blue towers from a distance; open daily 10:00-24:00; bus #11 from Rossio) for its more than 300 shops, piles of eateries, and theaters.

Lisbon at Night

From the Baixa, nighttime Lisbon seems dead. But head up into the Baírro Alto and you'll find lots of action. The Jardim do São Pedro is normally festive and the Rua Diario de Noticias is lined with bars. For entertainment specifics, pick up a copy of the periodical, *Se7e.* ("Sete" means 7.)

Lisbon reels with theaters and, unlike Spain, most films are in the original language with subtitles. Many of Lisbon's more than 90 theaters are classy, complete with assigned seats and ushers, and every day is a bargain day.

Sleeping in Lisbon, telephone code: 01, see postal codes below.

Finding a room in Lisbon is easy. Cheap and charming ride the same teeter-totter. If you arrive late, or in August, the room-finding services in the station and at the airport are helpful. Most of my listings fill up every night in August but will hold a room for a phone call. Classier places fill up first, especially in October, the convention season. Most of the year you can just wander through the district of your choice and find your own bed. If you have a room reserved, take a taxi from the station.

Many pensions ($20-$50 doubles) are around the Rossio and in the side streets near the Avenida Liberdade. Quieter and more colorful places are in the Baírro Alto and around the Castelo São Jorge. These areas seem a little sleazy at night but, with adequate caution, are not dangerous. You may see a few prostitutes but, unless you eyeball them, they'll ignore you.

When searching for a pension, remember: singles are nearly the cost of doubles; a building may contain several different pensions; addresses like 26-3 mean street #26, third floor (which is fourth floor in American terms). And never judge a place by its entryway. Remember, prices for rooms are listed by general range: doubles under $22 are "very cheap"; from $22 to $33 are "cheap"; from $33 to

$55 are "inexpensive"; $55 to $80 are "moderate"; over $80 are "expensive."

Rooms Downtown (Baixa and Rossio Area, postal code: 1100): This area is as central, safe, and bustling as possible in Lisbon, with lots of shops, traffic, people, police, pedestrian areas, and urban intensity. I've listed places that are in relatively quiet areas or on pedestrian streets. From the Rossio station, exit straight out the level on which you arrive, bypass the taxis, then veer right and up to Sacramento.

Pensão Coimbra e Madrid (inexpensive, right on Praça da Figueira at #3, third floor, no elevator, tel. 342-1760, English spoken) is family-run and high above the noise and ambience of a great square.

Pensão Norte (cheap, Rua dos Douradores 159, just off Praça da Figueira and Rossio, tel. 87 89 41 or 42) has an elevator, is friendly, central, plain and clean, but no one speaks English.

Hotel Duas Nacões (inexpensive-moderate, Rua Augusta e Rua da Vitoria 41, 1100 Lisbon, tel. 346 2082) is my best-value normal hotel listing. This fine old hotel is located in the heart of Rossio and on a classy pedestrian street. Some rooms without a shower give those with Hilton tastes and youth hostel budgets a workable compromise.

Hotel Suisso Atlantico (moderate, Rua da Gloria 3-19, behind the funicular station, around the corner from the tourist office on a quiet street one block off Praça dos Restauradores, tel. 346-1713, fax 346 9013) has a perfect location. It's formal, hotelish, and a bit stuffy, with lots of tour groups and depressing carpets throughout, but it has decent rooms and a TV lounge. If you want a functional hotel and practical location, and can ignore the floor, it's a good value.

Rooms in the Chiado and Baírro Alto, postal code 1200: Just west of downtown, this area is more colorful with less traffic. It's a bit seedy but full of ambience, good bars, local fado clubs, music, and markets. The area may not feel comfortable for women alone at night, but the hotels themselves are safe.

The newly renovated **Residencial Nova Silva** (inexpensive, no elevator, Rua Victor Cordón 11, 1200 Lisboa, tel. 342-4371, fax 342-7770) has a fine location between Baírro Alto and the river, providing some great river views. The owner, English-speaking Shamina, and her staff are very helpful. It's often full, so call well in advance and reconfirm two days early. Rooms with a view are given to those who stay longest, but ask anyway. Located in a quiet, well-guarded governmental district three minutes toward the river from the heart of Chiado on the scenic #28 tram line. Easiest street parking of all my listings.

Residencial Camões (inexpensive, Trav. Poco da Cidade 38, one block in front of São Roque Church and to the right, you'll see the sign, tel. 346-7510, fax 346 4048) lies right in the seedy thick of the Baírro Alto but maintains a bright, cheery atmosphere and very safe feeling. It's friendly, with great rooms, and English is spoken.

Pensão Duque (dirt cheap, Calçada do Duque 53, tel. 346-3444) has a great location on the pedestrian stairway street just off Largo Trinidade at the edge of Baírro Alto, up from Rossio. English is spoken by a friendly staff (ask for Lew-weez). This place, with an ancient tangle of steep stairways, tacky vinyl floors, yellow paint, and dim lights, is too seedy for most, but will be renovated soon. The price, location, hard beds, and saggy ancient atmosphere, however, make it a prize for some. Water and just about everything but the bed are down the hall.

Hotel Borges (expensive, Rua Garrett 108, on the shopping street next to A Braziliera café, tel. 346-1951, fax 342 6617) is a decent Old World hotel splurge.

Rooms in the Alfama, Uptown, and farther out: Pensão Ninho das Aguias (inexpensive, Rua Costa do Costselo 74, tel. 886 7008) is just under the castle, with great city views, a pleasant garden and a neon sign directing you there.

York House, also called **Residencia Inglesa** (22,000$ including everything, Rua Janeles Verdes 32, tel. 396-2435, fax 397 2793), is the choice of every expert on Lisbon . . . if you're loaded. Out toward Belem district, this renovated sixteenth-century convent is popular for its pleasant English atmosphere in an old villa with a garden.

To enjoy a more peaceful, old-resort atmosphere away from the big-city intensity, establish headquarters at Cascais, or at Sintra, just a few miles away. Cheap, 30-minute trains go downtown several times an hour.

Eating in Lisbon

Alfama: This gritty chunk of pre-earthquake Lisbon is full of interesting eateries, especially along the Rua San Pedro (the main drag) and on Largo de São Miguel. For a fancy meal (2,500$) after your Alfama exploration, eat at the gleaming blue-tiled restaurant, called **Miradouro de Santa Lucia**, just across from the patio view point overlooking the Alfama. A good splurge in this area, with a harbor view, is the **Faz O Figura** (expensive, Rua do Paraíso 15B, call 886 89 81 for reservations). For the real thing, cheap and colorful, walk behind the Miradouro de Santa Luzia to **Largo Rodrigues Freitas**. This hard-to-find square and the steepest lane down from it have plenty of very local eateries with 500$ meals.

While in the Alfama, brighten a few dark bars. Have an aperitif, taste the *branco seco* (local dry white wine). Make a friend, pet a chicken, read the graffiti, pick at the humanity ground between the cobbles. On the edge of the Alfama, just up the road from the Rossio, the **Cantinho do Aziz**, run by friendly Aziz and his wife, Felida, serves great Mozambique BBQ chicken in a homey setting.

Baírro Alto: Lisbon's "old town" is full of small, fun, and cheap places. Fishermen's bars line the Rua Nova Trinidade. Deeper into the Baírro Alto, past Rua Misericordia, you'll find the area's best meals. The **Cervejareía da Trinidade** at Rua Nova da Trinidade 20C (tel. 342-3506) is a Portuguese-style beer hall, covered with great tiled walls and full of fish and locals. You'll remember a dinner here.

Between Chiado and the river (next to recommended Residencial Nova Silva), just off Rua Victor Cordón at Travessado Ferragial 1, is a colorful self-service restaurant run by the Catholic church, with a very local feel, great food, impossibly cheap prices, and a river-view terrace (open Monday-Friday, 12:00-15:00, closed August).

Rossio and Baixa (lower town): The "eating lane"—just off Praça dos Restauradores down Rua do Jardim do Regedor and Rua das Portas de Santo Antão—is a galloping gourmet's heaven with a galaxy of eateries with small zoos hanging from their windows to choose from. The seafood is some of Lisbon's best. Rather than siesta, have a small black coffee (called a *bica*) in a shady café on the Avenida Liberdade. The nearby **express supermarket** on the rua Regedor is open late and on Sundays.

For a meal faster than a Big Mac and served with more energy than a soccer team, stand or sit at the **Restaurant/Cervejaría Beira-Gare** (in front of the Rossio station at the end of Rua 1 de Dezembro). If you're on the run, eat at the bar amid sliding beers and coins slam-dunked into the cash register.

In the Rossio are plenty of local favorites along Rua dos Correiros (like **Restaurant X** at #116; look for the red X). On the stairway up from rua Duque, try the very simple and cheap Casa Trans-Montanta. In the suburb of Belem, you'll find several good restaurants along Rua de Belem between the coach museum and the monastery.

Not so central: O Policia, Rua Marquesa de Bandeira 112 (an easy taxi ride from the center, just behind the Gulbenkian Museum, tel. 352 7060), has great local food, an interesting scene, and very good service by an entire academy of cute cops (at least they dress like cops). Open Monday-Friday 12:00-15:00, 19:00-22:00, Saturday 12:00-16:00; moderate prices. For tasty food and an even tastier view try **Restaurante O Marinheiro** (the sign says "Cooperative") west of Chiado near the Jardim Santa Catarina, tel 347 25 52.

For dinner in Estrela (end of tram #28, near the entry to Estrela Park), try **Flor D'Estrela** for good atmosphere, local music, and fine food.

If you feel like sailing to dinner, catch a frequent ferry from Praça do Comércio to the port town of Cacilhas, famous for its top-notch fish restaurants. For a special splurge, cross the bridge and turn right to find **Floresta do Ginjal** (7 Ginjal, tel. 275-0087).

Finally, don't miss a chance to go purely local with hundreds of Portuguese families having salad, fries, chicken, and wine at the Feira Popular.

Coffee and Port: Coffeehouse aficionados should not miss Lisbon's grand old café, **A Brasiliera** (Rua Garret 122, in the heart of Chiado), reeking with smoke and the 1930s. If you're into port, (the fortified wine that takes its name from the city of Oporto), you'll find the world's greatest selection nearby at **Solar do Vinho do Porto** (run by the Port Wine Institute, Rua São Pedro de Alcantara 45, top of the funicular, 10:00 to 23:45, closed Sunday). In a stuffy 60's-decor living-room atmosphere you can, for a price, taste any of 250 different ports, though you may want to try only 125 or so and save the rest for the next night. Fans of port describe it as "a liquid symphony playing on the palate."

DAY 10

LISBON SIDE TRIP TO BELÉM, SINTRA, AND THE ATLANTIC COAST

Sail through Portugal's seafaring glory days with a morning in the suburb of Belém; then spend the afternoon touring the Versailles of Portugal, climbing through a windy, desolate, ruined Moorish castle, and exploring the rugged and picturesque westernmost tip of Portugal. Mix and mingle with the jet set (or at least press your nose against their windows) at the resort towns of Cascais or Estoril before returning to Lisbon.

Suggested Schedule—By Car	
8:00	Breakfast, buy picnic lunch.
9:00	Trolley or drive to Belém.
10:00	Tour Belém to see the glories of Lisbon's Golden Age. Picnic at Belém Tower or lunch on Rua de Belém.
14:00	Drive to Sintra, tour Pena Palace, explore the ruined Moorish castle (great picnic spot if you rush Belém).
17:00	Drive out to Cabo da Roca.
18:00	Evening in resort of Estoril or Cascais, or back in Lisbon. Or, if you're itchy for the beach, you could drive five hours tonight direct from Sintra.

The Route: Circular Excursion, Lisbon-Belém-Sintra-Cabo da Roca-Cascais-Lisbon (about 70 miles)
Except for the traffic congestion around Sintra, this trip is easy and most fun by car. Follow the coast from Praça do Comércio west, under the bridge to Belém. Continue west to just before Cascais where Sintra (11 km) is signposted.

By Bus and Train
Take the trolley to Belém (#15, #16 or #17 from Praça Commercio) and spend your morning there. Very frequent train service from Lisbon makes Sintra and Cascais easy

afternoon trips (45-minute one-way trip to Sintra from Rossio station, 40 minutes to Cascais from Cais do Sodre station). Buses connect Sintra and Cascais (1-hour trip, the bus stop is across the street from the Sintra train station). Connecting Sintra and Cabo da Roca is tough without hitching. Without a car, I'd skip Cabo da Roca and do Sintra, Cascais, and Belém as individual side trips from Lisbon.

▲▲▲Belém

The Belém District, three miles from downtown Lisbon, is a pincushion of important sights from Portugal's Golden Age, when Vasco da Gama and company made it Europe's richest power. This is the best look possible at the grandeur of pre-earthquake Lisbon. You can get there by taxi or bus, but I'd ride the trolley (#15, #16, #17 from Praça do Comércio).

The Belém Tower, the only purely Manueline building in Portugal (built in 1515), protected Lisbon's harbor and today symbolizes the voyages that made it powerful. This was the last sight sailors saw as they left and the first one they'd see when they returned loaded down with gold, diamonds, spices, and social diseases. Its collection of fifteenth- and sixteenth-century armaments is barely worth the admission, but if you do go in, climb up for the view (open Tuesday-Sunday 10:00-13:30 and 14:30-17:00).

Belém

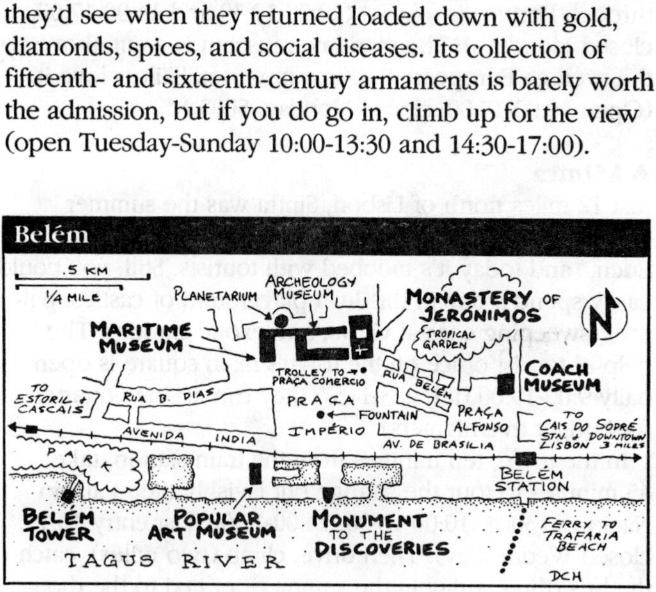

The giant Monument to the Discoveries was built in 1960 to honor Prince Henry the Navigator, who died 500 years earlier. Huge statues of Henry and Portugal's leading explorers line the giant concrete prow. Note the marble map chronicling Portugal's expansion on the ground in front. Inside you can ride a lift to a fine view (300$).

The Monastery of Jerónimos is, for me, Portugal's most exciting building. In the giant church and its cloisters, notice how nicely the Manueline style combines Gothic and Renaissance features with motifs from the sea, the source of wealth that made this art possible. Don't miss the elegant cloisters—my favorite in Europe (open 10:00-13:00 and 14:30-17:00, closed Monday, 500$). Go upstairs for a better view.

The Belém museums are somewhere between good and mediocre, depending on your interests. The Museu dos Coches (coach museum), claiming be to the most visited sight in Portugal, is most impressive with over 70 dazzling carriages from the eighteenth century (500$, 10:00-17:30, until 18:30 in summer, closed Monday, tel. 363-8164). The popular art museum takes you one province at a time through Portugal's folk art (10:00-12:30 and 14:00-17:00, closed Mondays). The maritime museum is a cut above the average European maritime museum. Sailors love it. (Open 10:00-17:00, closed Monday, 500$.)

▲▲Sintra

Just 12 miles north of Lisbon, Sintra was the summer escape of Portugal's kings. Byron called it a "glorious Eden," and today it's mobbed with tourists. Still, you could easily spend a day in this lush playground of castles, palaces, sweeping coastal views, and exotic gardens. The helpful tourist office on the town's main square is open daily 9:00-19:00 (tel. 923-1157; they can arrange quartos for budget overnighters).

In the town, ten minutes from the train station, take 45 minutes to tour the strange but lavishly tiled Palacio Nacional (300$, 10:00-13:00, 14:00-17:00, last entry 16:15, closed Wednesday). Then drive, climb (two miles), catch the bus (three a day in the summer), or taxi to the thou-

Lisbon Region

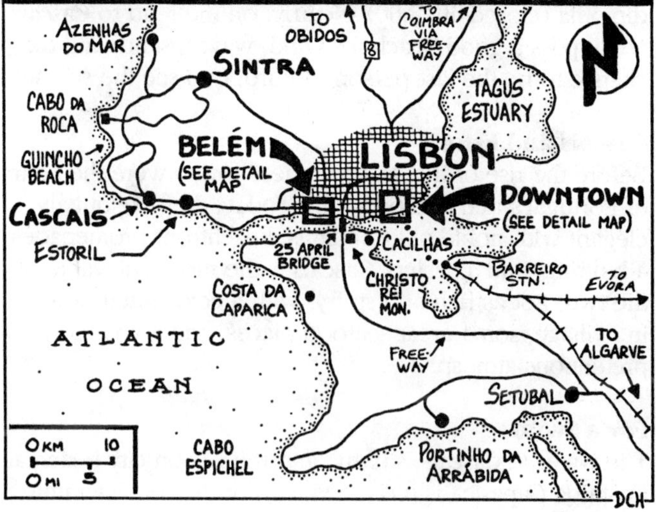

sand-year-old Moorish castle ruins (Castelo dos Mouros). Lost in an enchanted forest and alive with winds of the past, these ruins are a castle-lover's dream come true and a great place for a picnic with a panoramic Atlantic view.

A drive or walk away is the magical hilltop Pena Palace (Palacio da Pena). Portugal's German-born Prince Ferdinand hired a German architect to build him a fantasy castle mixing elements of German and Portuguese style. He got a crazy fortified casserole of Gothic, Arabic, Moorish, Walt Disney, Renaissance, and Manueline architectural bits and decorative pieces. The palace, built in the 1840s, is preserved just as it was when the royal family fled Portugal in 1910. For a spectacular view of Lisbon and the Tagus, hike for 15 minutes from the palace to the chapel of Santa Eufemia (you'll see signs; 300$, open 10:00-13:00 and 14:00-17:00, closed Monday).

Also in the area is the wonderful garden of Monserrate. If you like tropical plants and exotic landscaping, this is definitely for you, (100$, open 10:00-17:30).

Cabo da Roca

The wind-beaten, tourist-infested Cabo da Roca is the westernmost point in Europe. It has a fun little shop, a café, and a tiny Turismo that sells a "proof of being here" diploma (closed at 18:00). Nearby, on the road to Cascais, you'll pass a good beach for wind, waves, sand, and the chance to be the last person in Europe to see the sun set.

Cascais and Estoril

Before the rise of the Algarve, these towns were the haunt of Portugal's rich and beautiful. Today, they are quietly elegant with noble old buildings, beachfront promenades, a bullring, and a casino. Cascais is the more enjoyable of the two, not as rich and stuffy, with a cozy touch of fishing village, some great seafood places, and a younger, less pretentious atmosphere.

For a Swim

The water at Cascais is filthy, and the Lisbon city beach at Costa da Caparica is too crowded. For the best swimming around, drive (public transportation is difficult) 30 miles south to the golden beaches, shell-shaped bay, restaurants, and warm, clean water at Port Portinho da Arrabida. Or, better yet, wait for the Algarve

DAY 11

LISBON TO THE ALGRAVE

Trade the big city for a sleepy fishing village on the south coast and a chance to enjoy Portugal's best beach. The route can be fast and direct, or you can detour inland to tour historic Évora and explore the Portuguese interior's dusty droves of olive groves and scruffy seas of peeled cork trees. The Algarve is the south coast of any sun worshiper's dreams. It's so good, I'd get there pronto. Your Algarve hideaway and goal for the day is the fishing village of Salema.

Suggested Schedule—By Car	
9:00	Depart, drive over 25th of April Bridge.
10:00	Go to top of Cristo Rei for a great view of Lisbon.
11:00	Drive or train south to Salema.
16:00	Set up in Salema, dinner on beach.
Note: Saturdays at 16:00, bullfights in Lagos.	

The Route: Lisbon to Salema (150 miles, 5 hours)
Following the blue "Sul Ponte" signs, drive south over Lisbon's 25th of April Bridge. A short detour just over the bridge takes you to the giant concrete Christ in Majesty statue. Then continue south past Setubal and follow N120 (signs to: Setubal, Alcacer, Algarve, Faro, Grandola, Sines, Cercal, Odemira, Vila do Bispo, Sagres, Lagos, Salema) to the south coast.

Along the way you'll pass the likable riverside town of Alcacer do Sal and grove after grove of cork trees with their telltale peeled trunks. After Grandola you could take a side trip to Praia de Melides, an ugly shanty town with lots of private rooms for rent and a beautiful sandy beach. Just south of Melides and right on the road you can take a walk along some coastal sand dunes and have a snack at Costa de Santo Andre. Just east of Vila do Bispo you'll hit Figueira and the tiny dirt road to the beach village of Salema. Decent roads and less traffic make doing this drive at night a reasonable option. The Algarve has good roads and lots of traffic.

By Bus and Train

I like the night train because it arrives early, allowing you to enjoy the entire day on the Algarve, but be aware that the 7-hour boat-train connection involves two changes and isn't too convenient. If you insist on daytime travel, both bus and train take about 5 hours to Lagos, but the train is more comfortable for this long trip. Trains from Lisbon to the south coast leave from the Barreiro station across the Tagus from downtown. Boats shuttle train travelers from Praça Comercio to the Barreiro station with several departures each hour (free with Eurailpass, 30-minute ride, note that schedule times listed are often when the boat sails, not when train departs). Rodoviaria express buses must be booked ahead of time (get details at the tourist office). They leave from Casal Ribiero 18, metro Picos, tel. 57 77 15.

Train service between the main towns along the south coast is excellent (nearly hourly between Lagos and the Spanish border) and buses will take you where the trains don't. Lagos is the nearest train station to Salema, a 15-kilometer hitch or bus ride away (ignore Lagos's "quartos women" who will tell you it's 50 kilometers away). From Lagos' train station, walk straight out, cross the bridge and then the main boulevard, and walk right into the bright yellow EVA bus station. Pick up return bus schedules and train schedules to Seville (via Villa Real) before you leave (note: bus stops are also on the waterfront if you venture into Lagos). Buses go almost hourly from Lagos to Sagres (60-minute ride), about half of which go right into the village of Salema—the others drop you at the top of its dead-end road, a 20-minute walk downhill into the village. If you arrive late in Lagos, consider one of its many inexpensive rooms for rent or try the luxurious youth hostel (read ahead).

Option: Évora and the Interior

With more time, you can visit Évora and Portugal's wild but sleepy interior. The villages you'll pass through in southern Alentejo are poor, quiet, and, in many cases, dying. Unemployment here is so bad that many locals have left their hometowns for jobs—or the hope of jobs—in the big city. This is the land of the "black widows," women whose husbands have abandoned them in search of work.

Évora

Évora has been a cultural oasis in the barren, arid plains of the southern province of Alentejo for 2,000 years. With a beautifully untouched provincial atmosphere, fascinating whitewashed old quarter, plenty of museums, a cathedral, and even a Roman temple, Évora stands proud amid groves of cork and olive trees.

The major sights (Roman temple of Diana, early Gothic cathedral, archbishop's palace, and a luxurious pousada in a former monastery) crowd close together at the town's highest point. Osteophiles eat up the macabre "House of Bones" chapel at the Church of St. Francis. It's lined with the bones of 5,000 monks. A subtler but still powerful charm is contained within the town's medieval wall. Find it by losing yourself in the quiet lanes of Évora's far corners.

The tourist offices are at Praça do Giraldo 73 (tel. 066/22671, open 9:00-19:00 Monday-Friday, a little less on weekends) and at the city entrance on the highway from Lisbon. For budget eating and sleeping, look around the central square, Praça do Giraldo. For a splurge, sleep in one of Portugal's most luxurious pousadas, the Convento dos Loios (across from the Roman temple, tel. 066/24051, expensive). I ate well for a moderate price at O Fialho (Travessa Mascarhenas 14). For very local atmosphere, eat at the "Restaurant" restaurant just off the Praça at 11 Rua Romano Romalha.

From Évora, drivers head south to Beja, west to Aljustrel, then south by any number of equal routes. The fastest is to follow the signs southwest to Odemira, then turn south toward Albufeira. All the roads are a mix of straight and winding, well-paved and washboard, and you'll spend your share of time in third gear.

Beja is nothing special. Its castle has a military museum (open 10:00-13:00 and 14:00-18:00) and a territorial view, and the old town is worth a look and a cup of coffee.

A more enjoyable stop on your drive south would be for a refreshing swim in one of the lonely lakes of the Alentejo Desert, such as Baragem do Maranho or Baragem do Montargil.

Plan on arriving at the resort town of Lagos on the southern coast by 18:00. From here, drive west about halfway to Cape Sagres, then hang a left and head down to the humble beach town of Salema.

Salema

See Day 12.

DAY 12

FREE ALGARVE BEACH DAY, SAGRES

Today will be a day of rigorous rest and intensive relaxation on the beaches of Salema, with a short side trip to explore Portugal's windy "land's end," Cape Sagres.

Suggested Schedule

By Car or Bus

10:00	Explore Cape Sagres and Cape St. Vincent.
13:00	Lunch and afternoon on Salema beach, seeing how slow you can get your pulse. Speedy ones can spend the afternoon in Lagos.

The Algarve

The Algarve, Portugal's southern coast, has long been known as Europe's last undiscovered tourist frontier. That statement, like "jumbo shrimp" and "military intelligence," contradicts itself. The Algarve is well discovered and most of it is going the way of the Spanish Costa del Sol—paved, packed, and pretty stressful. It's actually overdeveloped with giant condo-type "villas" hovering over just about every beach that has road access. There is a sizable community of expatriates—mostly British. For an English-language peek into the "ex-pat" scene pick up a copy of the *Algarve News*.

Salema

One bit of old Algarve magic still glitters quietly in the sun—Salema. You'll find it at the end of a small road just off the main drag between the big city of Lagos and the rugged southwest tip of Europe, Cape Sagres. This simple fishing village, quietly discovered by British and German tourists, is the best beach town left on the Algarve. It has a few hotels, time-share condos up the road, some hippies' bars with rock music, English and German menus and signs (bullfight ads for "Stierkampf"), a classic beach, and endless sun.

The Algarve

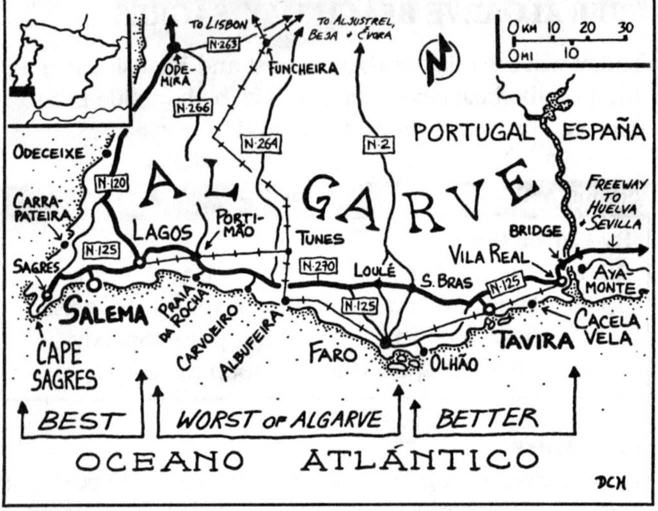

Salema has a flatbed truck market that rolls in each morning—one truck for fish, one for fruit, one for vegetables, and one for clothing and other odds and ends. A highlight of any Salema day is watching the fishing boats come and go (a tractor drags them in). Some bring in pottery jars from the ocean's bottom. Octopi inhabit them and are hauled in—the last mistake they'll ever make. Salema is most crowded in July, August, and September, when local boats offer scenic trips along the coast. Boycott the Restaurant O Pereira, whose owner built the giant white monstrosity two floors higher than the code limits. It's a sledgehammer of ugliness in the heart of Salema. Telephone code: 082.

Sleeping in Salema, telephone code: 082, postal code: 8650, Algarve.
Lying where a dirt road hits the sea, Salema has three streets, five restaurants, a couple of bars, a lane full of fisherfolk who happily rent out rooms to foreign guests, and an ever-growing circle of modern condo-type hotels, apartments, and villas up the hillside.

I'd skip the hotels and go for the quartos (bed-and-breakfast places). At the waterfront ask one of the locals, or ask at the Boia Bar or the mini-market for quartos. There are plenty of private homes renting rooms along the town's residential street, which runs left from the village center as you face the beach. Prices vary dramatically with the season but are always cheap (4000$ maximum for doubles). While my last room came with a bed pan, there's usually adequate plumbing (sometimes with hot water only in the evening). Many places offer beachfront balconies or views. Few of the locals speak English, but

Salema, Algarve Hideaway

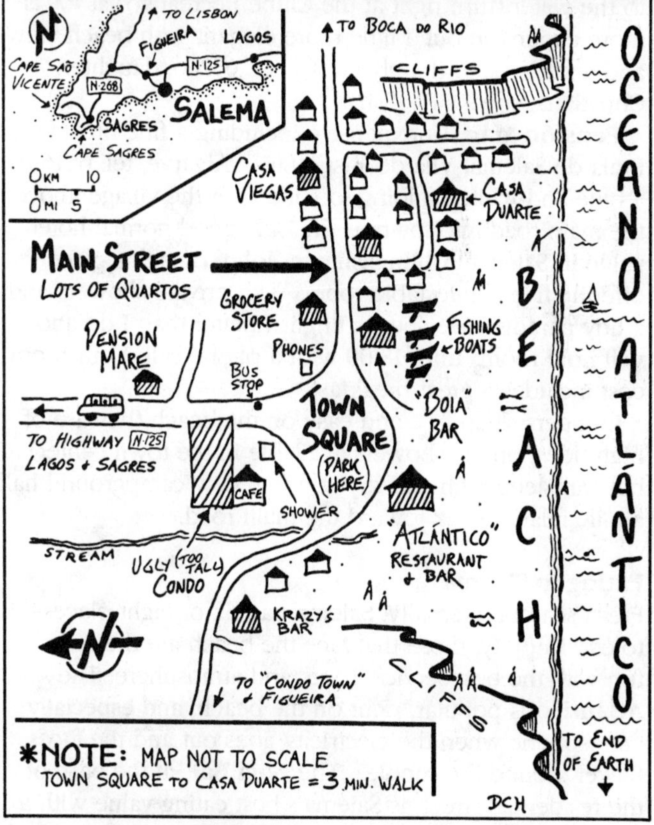

they're used to dealing with visitors. Many of the quartos' landladies will happily clean your laundry, also cheap.

The only sizable place on the "quartos street" is the brown-tiled building, #64. The home of Romeu and Ercilia Viegas has seven inexpensive doubles; none have sinks, but there is a communal kitchenette and one bathroom on the pleasant sun terrace (cheap, tel. 65128; they speak no English, but their daughter, Selinha, who lives in Lisbon, tel. 253 3375, does, and she can arrange a room for you). The **Acacios** at #91 just entered the quarto buisness with two good rooms; the upstairs room is far better with a balcony and great ocean view. No English spoken (tel. 65473).

The **Casa Duarte**, farther up and on a side alley closer to the water (turn right at the Clube Recreativo) at #7, is more expensive but a little more elegant with beach views and a kitchenette (barely cheap, tel. 65206; daughter, Christiana, speaks English).

Pensión Mare (inexpensive including a fine breakfast; Praia de Salema, Vila do Bispo 8650, Algarve, tel. 65165), a blue-and-white building looking over the village above the main road into town, is the only good normal hotel value in Salema. An Englishman, John, runs this place offering five comfortable rooms with private showers and a tidy paradise. He speaks English better than I do and will hold rooms until 18:00 with a phone call. Your room cost includes a great breakfast.

Campers sleep free and easy on the beach (beware of high tides; public showers available in the town center) but can sleep high and dry at a fine new campground half a mile inland, back toward the main road.

Eating in Salema

Fresh seafood eternally. Salema has six or eight places to eat. Happily, those that face the beach are the most fun with the best service, food, and atmosphere. The **Atlantico** is popular, right on the beach, and especially atmospheric when the electricity goes out and the faces flicker around the candles. The **Boia Bar**, at the base of the residential street, is Salema's best eating value with a few tables within splashing distance of the surf, good tunes, huge portions, and a hearty loss leader breakfast giving you the bacon, eggs, toast, coffee, and fresh-squeezed orange juice works for the cost of two glasses of OJ anywhere else in town.

Figueira

You missed the untouristed Salema by about five years. For a less glamorous and less touristy option, stay in the town of Figueira, a mile from Salema and the water, where old men still whittle.

Merryl and "Rev" Revill, more British expatriates, run **Casa Meranka**, a charming guest house with ten rooms and a pool, 20 minutes walk from your own private beach in a town that is still as local as it was in the days when the Algarve was truly undiscovered. They serve breakfast in the garden, can arrange jeep safaris to the remote interior, and are a wealth of local information (inexpensive with breakfast; Rua do Rossio, Figueira 8650 Vila do Bispo, tel. 082/65303; call a few days in advance if possible). The **Sapinho** restaurant, across the street, is the place for a reasonable meal in Figueira.

Cape Sagres

From Salema it's a short drive or hitch or a half-hour bus trip (several daily trips from Salema, check return times!) to the rugged and historic southwestern tip of Portugal. This was the spot closest to the edge of our flat earth in the days before Columbus. Prince Henry the Navigator, who was determined to broaden Europe's horizons, sent sailors ever farther into the unknown and had a navigator's school at Cape Sagres. Henry lived here, carefully debriefing shipwrecked and frustrated explorers as they washed ashore.

Today, fishermen cast from its towering crags, local merchants sell seaworthy sweaters ($20), and the windswept landscape harbors sleepy beaches, a salty village, and the lavish Pousada do Infante. For a touch of local elegance, pop by the pousada for breakfast. For 1,000$ you can sip coffee and nibble on a still-warm croissant while gazing out to where, in the old days, the world dropped right off the table. The **Pousada**, a reasonable splurge offering a classy hotel in a magnificent setting (16,000$ doubles, Pousada do Infante, 8650 Sagres, tel. 082/64222, fax 64225), offers a warm welcome to anyone ready to pay so much for a continental breakfast.

Sagres is a popular gathering place for the backpacking crowd with plenty of private rooms available right in town. The beach and bar scene are great for the *Let's Go* crowd.

The best secluded beach in the region is Praia da Castelejo, just north of Cape Sagres (from Villa do Bispo, turn inland and follow the signs for 15 minutes). For a 2.5-hour fishing-boat trip from Salema to Sagres and back with possible swimming stops at desolate beaches, catch a ride with Sebastian (educational, bird-watching, etc.) or Marcolino (less predictable and as trippy as you like it). Both charge about 2000$ per person.

DAY 13

ACROSS THE ALGARVE, BACK INTO SPAIN, TO SEVILLA

If your solar cells are recharged, it's time to hit the road again. You'll make a few short Algarve stops, then cross the new bridge to Spain and on to Sevilla, the city of flamenco.

Suggested Schedule—By Car	
9:00	Depart Salema after breakfast.
10:00	Stroll through Lagos (if you didn't yesterday).
11:00	Drive to Tavira.
13:00	Lunch and browse in Tavira.
15:00	Drive to Sevilla (set clock ahead one hour).
18:00	Arrive in Sevilla. First stop: tourist office. Set up in hotel.

The Route: Algarve to Sevilla (150 miles)
Drive east along the Algarve. In Lagos, park along the waterfront by the fort (and Mobil gas station). To avoid traffic, take the inland route, following signs to Faro, then Loule, to Tavira. It's a 2-hour drive from Salema to Tavira. Leaving Tavira, follow signs to V. Real, then España. The long-awaited bridge is now complete, so you'll zip effortlessly into Spain. It's about 90 minutes by freeway to Sevilla. At Sevilla, follow the signs to Centro Ciudad (city center), drive along the river, and park (at least to get set up) near the cathedral and tower. You'll also see signs to the the Prado de San Sebastian, a huge centrally located parking lot.

By Bus and Train *Caution: Sunday bus service is drastically reduced.*
Salema to Seville is a long and somewhat-confusing day by bus and train, though it does work. Call the Lagos Turismo for transport information (tel: 082/ 76 30 31); English is spoken. Lagos' train information tel. is 082/76 2987. Take an early moring bus to Lagos (I walked up

to the main road to catch the Sagres-Lagos express bus). Take the train to the last stop in Villa Real de San Antonio (several good morning departures; allow 4.5 hours with a possible transfer in Faro) which connects directly to a river-crossing ferry (150$) to the pleasant Spanish border town of Ayamonte. From the Ayamonte dock, walk through the town (angling slightly to the right) and find the bus stop next to the main square (shops take escudos and banks convert change into pesetas). Buses depart irregularly to Seville (catch one if you can) and more regularly for the uninteresting city Huelva (1 hour), where you can connect to another bus or train to Seville (both take about 1.5 hours, but buses run more frequently). The Huelva train station is about a 15 minute-walk from the bus station (turn left out of the station, take the first right, then left onto the first main boulevard, which leads to the station).

From the Seville bus station, turn right on Carlos V and walk straight to Ave. Constitucion to reach the city center. Leaving Seville's impressive new Santa Justa train station, make a hard left and catch bus #70 on the near side of the street to the cathedral. (Note: both the Cordoba and San Bernardo stations in Seville have been replaced by this one mega-station.)

Algarve Sightseeing Highlights

▲Lagos—The major town and high-rise resort on this end of the Algarve is actually a pleasant place. The old town around the Praça Infante D. Henrique and the fort is a whitewashed jumble of bars, funky craftshops, outdoor restaurants, and sunburned tourists. The church of San Antonio and the adjoining regional museum are worth a look. The beaches with the exotic rock formations (of postcard fame) are near the fort. Every summer Saturday at 16:00, Lagos has a small, for-tourists bullfight in its dinky ring. Seats are a steep 3,000$, but the show is a thriller. Lagos is understandably famous (and crowded) for its beautiful beaches and rugged cliffs. If you need a room, try the Club-Med-like youth hostel—it's new and very comfortable with many private rooms (cheap; rua

Lancorte de Freitas 50, 8600 Lagos, tel. 082/ 76 1970). Lagos' Tourismo is on the Largo Marques de Pombal, is loaded with information (bus and train schedules are posted), and is open from 9:30 to 20:00 weekdays, and until 17:30 on weekends. Tel: 082/ 76 30 31.

▲▲Tavira—Straddling a river, with a lively park, a`market, and boats in its waterfront center, Tavira is a low-rise, easygoing alternative to the other more aggressive Algarve resorts. It's your best east Algarve stop. Even for just a quick break, park near the Turismo and river to enjoy the park (Jardím, off Praça da República). Tavira has a great beach island (catch the bus to Quatro Aguas from Praça da República and then the 5-minute ferry ride to Ilha da Tavira). Off-season, the ferry sleeps. Those with a car can park at the bridge just after nearby Santa Lucia and walk (1 km) or catch the little train to Barril Beach.

Those without a car will find Tavira easier to manage than Salema, with a direct Lisbon train connection, an easier trip to Sevilla, and a still-good, if not so magic, small-townish Algarve atmosphere. The train station is a 10-minute walk from the town center.

Tavira has several good hotels. My favorite is the **Lagaos Bica** (cheap; Rua Almirante Candido dos Reis 24, 8800 Tavira, tel. 081/22252). This residencia is clean, homey, and a block off the river. The friendly English-speaking manager, Maria, offers a communal refrigerator, a rooftop patio with a view made for wine and candles, a courtyard garden, laundry washboard privileges, and a good restaurant downstairs. Also a good value is the more hotelesque **Residencia Princesa do Gilão**, which faces the river in the town center (inexpensive; Rua Borda de Agua de Aguiar, tel. 081/325171). It offers bright, cheery, modern rooms, some with balconies and a view, and an English-speaking management. **Pensão Castelo** (inexpensive; across from the Turismo at Rua da Liberdade 4, tel. 081/23942) is also good. The tourist office is open daily from 9:30 to 19:00 and can set you up in a 2,500$ double room in a private home (tel. 081/22511).

Cacela Velha—Just a few miles east of Tavira, this tiny village fell through the cracks. It sits on a hill with its fort, church, one restaurant, a few quartos, and a beach with the open sea just over the sandbar a short row across its lagoon. The restaurant serves a fried-at-your-table sausage-and-cheese specialty. It's just a minute off the main road. Drop by, if only to enjoy the coastal view and imagine how nice the Algarve would be if people like you and me never discovered it.

Sevilla

See Day 14.

DAY 14

SEVILLA

This is the city of flamenco, Carmen, and Don Juan. While Granada has the great Alhambra, Sevilla has a soul. It's a great-to-be-alive-in kind of place. Sevilla boomed when Spain did, the gateway to the New World. Explorers like Amerigo Vespucci and Magellan sailed from its great river harbor. Sevilla's Golden Age, with its New World riches and great local artists (Velázquez, Murillo, Zurbarán), ended when the harbor silted up and the Spanish Empire crumbled.

Today, Sevilla (pop. 700,000, Spain's fourth-largest city) is Andalusia's number-one city. It buzzes with festivals, life, and color. James Michener wrote, "Sevilla doesn't *have* ambience, it *is* ambience."

Suggested Schedule

9:00	Plaza Nueva, shopping, bullfight museum.
11:00	Cathedral and tower.
13:00	Lunch, siesta.
15:30	Alcázar and gardens.
17:00	Stroll Santa Cruz neighborhood and along the river (or tour Bellas Artes Museum and Macarena).

Evening: Relax at the hotel, stroll through the Barrio de Santa Cruz and up toward the Plaza Nueva for a nightly people parade. By then it's time to dine. Flamenco is best around midnight. Tourist shows start at 21:00; spontaneous combustion in bars at 23:00.

Note: Alcázar is closed Mondays; bullfights are most Sundays April through October.

Sevilla Orientation

For the tourist, this big city is small. Think of things relative to the river and the cathedral with its skyline-dominating tower, which is as central as you can get. The major sights, including the lively Santa Cruz district and the Alcázar, surround the cathedral. Parallel to the river, the

Sevilla

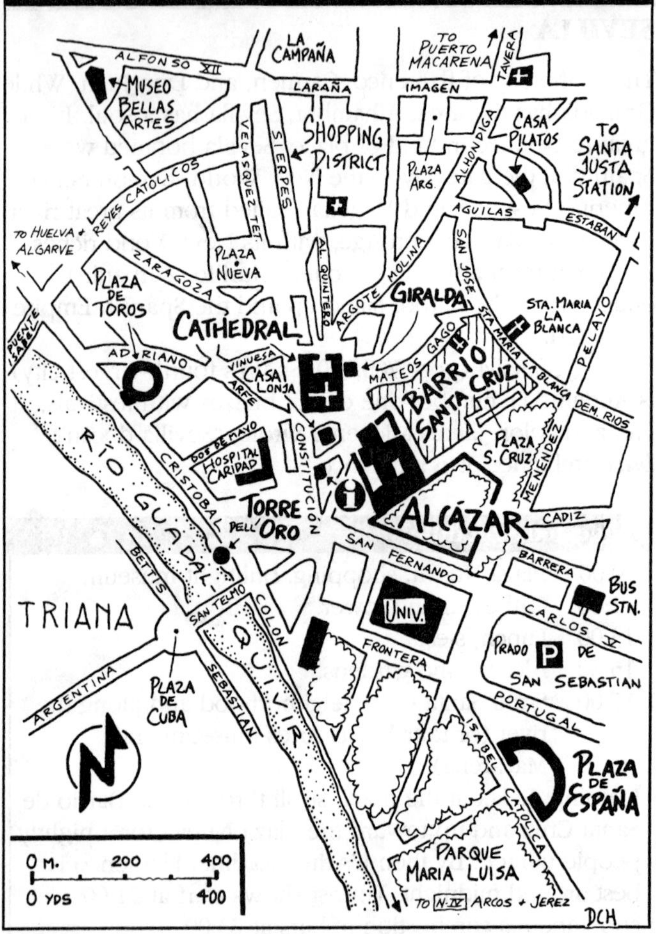

central boulevard, Avenida de la Constitución (tourist information, banks, post office, etc.), zips right past the cathedral to the Plaza Nueva (shopping district). Nearly everything is within easy walking distance. Taxis are reasonable (250 ptas minimum), friendly, and thrilling.

Sevilla is Spain's capital of splintered windshields. Many risk it and win. The more prudent pay to park in the garage near the bullring. The most reliable parking is in the huge pay lot (the Prado de San Sebastian) between the university and Plaza de España. Paseo de Cristobal Colón ("Christopher Columbus" in Spanish) also has free places but is particularly dangerous in the summer. Get advice from your hotel.

The "we try harder" tourist office is near the cathedral toward the river (open daily 9:30-19:30, Saturday 9:30-14:00, closed Sunday; tel. 422-1404). Pick up the Sevilla map/guide, ideas for evening fun, a map of Jerez, and *The Route of the White Towns* brochure, and confirm tomorrow's schedule. Train information: 41 41 11. All Sevilla phone numbers have seven digits now. Old numbers now start with a 4. Telephone code: 095. There are no buses to the airport, only taxis.

Sightseeing Highlights—Sevilla

▲Cathedral—This is the third-largest church in Europe (after St. Peter's and St. Paul's), the largest Gothic building anywhere. When the Catholics ripped down a mosque on the site in 1401, they bragged, "We'll build a cathedral so huge that anyone who sees it will take us for madmen." Even today, the descendants of those madmen proudly display several enlarged photocopies of their Guinness Book of Records letter certifying, "The cathedral with the largest area is: Santa Maria de la Sede in Sevilla, 126 meters long, 82 meters wide, and 30 meters high." (Guinness doesn't have an "ugliest cathedral" category.)

Take a hike through the royal chapel, the sanctuary, and the treasury, and don't miss Columbus' tomb (with the pallbearers, near the entry). The incredible *retablo* (paneled altarpiece) has 4,000 pounds of gold, imported in the "free trade" era (b. 1492), with 1,500 figures carved by one man over 40 years. In the *tesoro* (treasury), you'll see a graphic head of John the Baptist, the most valuable crown in Spain (11,000 precious stones and the world's largest pearl, made into the body of an angel), lots of relics (thorns, chunks of the cross, splinters from the Last Supper table), and some of the lavish Corpus Christi festival parade regalia (open 11:00-17:00, Saturday 11:00-16:00, Sunday 14:00-16:00; 500 ptas)

▲**Giralda Tower**—Formerly a Moorish minaret from which Muslims were called to prayer, it became the cathedral's bell tower after the Reconquista. Notice the beautiful Moorish simplicity as you climb to its top, 100 yards up, for a grand city view. The spiraling ramp is designed to accommodate riders on horseback, so gallop up the 34 ramps and orient yourself from this bird's-eye perspective (same hours, tickets, and entry as the cathedral).

▲▲▲**Alcázar**—What you'll see today is basically a palace built by Moorish workmen (*mudejar*) for the Christian King Pedro I, who was called either "the Cruel" or "the Just," depending on which end of the sword you were at. Like Granada's Alhambra, the Alcázar is a thought-provoking glimpse of a graceful Al-Andalus (Moorish) world that might have survived its Castilian conquerors . . . but didn't. The Alcázar is intentionally confusing (part of the style designed to make experiencing the place more exciting and surprising), with an impressive collection of royal courts, halls, patios, and apartments. In many ways it's as splendid as the more famous Alhambra. The garden is full of tropical flowers, wild cats, cool fountains, and hot tourists. Sit in the most impressive part of the palace and freeload on passing tours (open Tuesday-Saturday 10:30-17:30, Sunday 10:00-13:30, closed Monday, 600 ptas).

The disappointing Archivo de Indias (archive of the documents of the discovery and conquest of the New World in a palace called the Lonja) is across the street from the Alcázar (free; 10:00-13:00, closed Sunday).

▲▲**Barrio de Santa Cruz** (the old Jewish Quarter)—Even if it is a little over-restored, this classy world of lanes too narrow for cars, whitewashed houses with wrought-iron latticework, and *azulejo*-covered patios is a great refuge from the summer heat and bustle of Sevilla. Be prepared to get lost in this maze of tourist shops, small hotels, flamenco bars, and peaceful squares.

Hospital de la Caridad—Between the river and the cathedral is the charity hospital founded by the original Don Juan. One of history's great hedonists, his party was crashed by a vision that tuned him in to his own mortality. He paid for the construction of this hospital for the poor and joined the Brotherhood of Charity. Peek into the fine courtyard. On the left, the chapel has some gruesome art (above the door) illustrating how death is the great equalizer, and an altar sweet as only a Spaniard could enjoy (open 10:00-13:00, 15:30-18:00, Sunday 10:30-12:30 only; 200 ptas).

Torre del Oro/Naval Museum—This historic riverside "gold tower" once received the booty of the New World. Today it houses a mediocre little naval museum with lots of charts showing various knots, models of ships, dried fish, and an interesting mural of Sevilla in 1740 (100 ptas; 10:00-14:00, Saturday and Sunday 10:00-13:00, closed Monday).

University—Today's university was yesterday's *fabrica de tabacos* (cigar factory), which employed 10,000 young female *cigareras*—including Bizet's Carmen. It was the second-largest building in Spain, after El Escorial. Wander through its halls as you walk to the Plaza de España. The university's bustling café is a great place for cheap tapas, beer, wine, and conversation (open 8:00-21:00, Saturday 9:00-13:00, closed Sunday).

▲Museo de Bellas Artes—Sevilla's top collection of art has 50 Murillos and works by Zurbarán, El Greco, and Velázquez (Plaza Museo 9, turn right at the bridge after the Ponte Isabel, open Tuesday-Friday 10:00-14:00 and 16:00-19:00, Saturday and Sunday 10:00-14:00).

▲Virgen de la Macarena—This altarpiece statue of the Weeping Virgin, complete with crystal teardrops, is the darling of Sevilla's Holy Week processions. She's very beautiful (her weeping can be contagious). Tour the exhibits behind the altar and go upstairs for a closer peek at Mary (open 9:00-13:00 and 16:30-21:00; the treasury is open 9:30-12:30 and 16:30-19:30; 300 ptas). Taxi to just off Puerta Macarena.

▲Bullfights—The most artistic and traditional bullfighting in Spain is done in Sevilla, with fights on most Sundays, April through October (information: tel. 422-3152). You can now follow an English-speaking guide for 15 minutes through the strangely quiet and empty arena, its museum, and the chapel where the matador prays before the fight

(10:00-13:30 daily, except fight days; 200 ptas, skip the 100 pta info sheet).

▲Plaza de España—The square, the surrounding buildings, and the nearby María Luisa Park are the remains of a 1929 fair that crashed with the stock market. This delightful area, the epitome of world's fair-style building, is great for people-watching. Stroll along the canal. Check out the azulejo tiles (a trademark of Sevilla) that show historic scenes and maps from every corner of Spain.

A Private Tour? Don't book a normal bus sightseeing tour. Sevilla is definitely an on-foot town, and for the price of two seats on a lousy bus tour you can have your own private and excellent local guide. Isidoro Martinez keeps busy leading groups around Sevilla during the day but will give two-hour private historic walks in the evening for 5,000 ptas. To arrange a tour call him at home a few days in advance at 095/442-4533 or at his office, 422-4641.

▲▲Evening Paseo—Sevilla is a town meant for strolling. The areas along the river and around the Plaza Nueva thrive every non-winter evening. Spend some time rafting through this sea of humanity and don't miss the view of Seville by night on the other side of the river.

▲▲Flamenco—Flamenco is more than just foot-stomping, posing, and chomping on roses. This music-and-dance art form has its roots in the Gypsy and Moorish cultures. Even at a packaged "Flamenco Evening," sparks can fly. Here are some things to watch for: The men do most of the flamboyant machine-gun footwork. The women concentrate on graceful turns and a smooth shuffling step. Watch the musicians. Flamenco guitarists, with their lightning finger-roll strums, are among the best in the world. The intricate rhythms are set by castanets or the hand clapping (called *palmas*) of those who aren't dancing at the moment. In the raspy-voiced wails of the singers, you'll hear echoes of the Muslim call to prayer.

Like jazz, flamenco thrives on improvisation. Also like jazz, good flamenco is more than just technical proficiency. A singer or dancer with "soul" is said to have *duende*. Flamenco is a happening, with bystanders clapping along and egging on the dancers with whoops and shouts. Get into it.

For a tourist-oriented flamenco show, your hotel can get you nightclub show tickets for about 3,000 ptas, including a drink. The Turismo has a current listing. You can try **La Trocha** (Ronda de Capuchinos 23, tel. 435-5028, 21:00-2:00) or **Los Gallos** (Plaza de Santa Cruz 11, tel. 421-6981, nightly shows at 21:00 and 23:30). These prepackaged shows can be a bit sterile, but I find Los Gallos professional and riveting.

The best flamenco erupts spontaneously in bars throughout the old town. Just follow your ears in the Barrio de Santa Cruz. Calle Salados, near Plaza de Cuba across the bridge, is also good. Flamenco rarely rolls before midnight.

Shopping—The fine pedestrian street, Calle Sierpes, and the smaller lanes around it near the Plaza Nueva, are packed with people and shops. The street ends up at Sevilla's top department store, El Corte Inglés. While small shops close between 13:00 and 16:00 or 17:00, El Corte Inglés stays open (and air-conditioned) right through the siesta. It has a good but expensive restaurant.

Sleeping in Sevilla, telephone code: 095, postal code: 41004.

Sevilla has plenty of $30 to $50 doubles, though you may have to work a little to find one. The best neighborhoods are Santa Cruz (lots of hostales and fondas, traffic-free, great atmosphere) and within the triangle between the Córdoba station, the bullring, and the Plaza Nueva. The farther they are from the plaza, the cheaper they get.

Room rates jump way up during the two Sevilla fiestas (roughly December 20 to January 4 and April 23 to May 7). Otherwise, April, May, September, and October are busiest and most expensive. June, July, and August are cheaper, when countless rooms are empty. Many hotels have strict seasonal rates (in a normal year, fair dates and March 20-May 31 are high, September through mid-October medium, and the rest of the year low).

All my recommendations are wonderfully located, within a five-minute walk of the cathedral. The first six are in the touristic and characteristic old Jewish Quarter, the Barrio de Santa Cruz (with your back to the cathedral entrance, walk straight down Mateos Gaga to reach these). This area is not the cheapest, but it's handy as can be with the sights, flamenco, parking (see above), tapas bars, and Turismo all nearby.

The **Hostal Goya** (inexpensive-moderate, Mateos Gago 31, tel. 421-1170, fax 456-2988) is 2 minutes down the street from the cathedral, with good rooms and a cozy courtyard. Ground-floor rooms are noisy and stuffy.

Hostal Monreal (inexpensive, Rodrigo Caro 8, tel. 421-4166) is simple, clean, and very entrepreneurial, and gives you the sensation of climbing through a tile tree-house. Take the first right off Mateos Gago. Pass on the ground floor rooms.

The **Hotel Residencia Murillo** (expensive, Lope de Rueda 7, tel. 421-6095, fax 421-9616) is big, dripping with decoration, and in the heart of the Santa Cruz district. It's very hotelesque, with "Murillo palette" key chains. Follow the sign from Plaza Santa Cruz (their brochure has a prize-winning Barrio Santa Cruz map).

To reach the following four places, turn right off Mateos Gaga at Meson del Moro. After snaking your way a few blocks you'll come to a crafts shop on St. Theresa at Lope de Rueda, run by British expatriates **Paul and Caroline.** They rent two apartments by the night, each with three rooms that would be ideal for families, or small groups (inexpensive, no telephone, fax 421-7986). If they're full they can suggest other nearby good values. That's how I found the **Pensao St. Cruz** (at the end of Lope de Rueda, #12 St. Cruz) a fine small pension, with several rooms around a beautifully tiled courtyard (inexpensive rooms, expensive showers, be clear on the price, tel. 421-7695). The nearby **Hostal Toledo** (inexpensive, half a block off Plaza Santa Cruz at Santa Teresa 15, tel. 421-5335, English spoken) is family run and has ten rooms, all with showers.

Hotel Residencia Doña María (sky-high, Don Remondo 19, tel. 422-4990, fax 421-9546) is just off the cathedral square, Plaza Vírgen de los Reyes. This is a wonderful splurge. It brags "very modern but furnished in an ancient style" and has four-poster beds, armoires, and a rooftop swimming pool with a view of Giralda Tower.

Closer to the Avenida de la Constitución, near the Tourist Office, you'll find the **Hostal Arias** (inexpensive-moderate, Calle Mariana de Pineda 9, tel. 422-6840, fax 421-8389) is clean, quiet, and no-nonsense, with hard beds. All fifteen rooms are air-conditioned and have showers. The manager, Manuel Reina, speaks American. There's a cheap **Casa Huéspedes** around the corner. You'll pass the new **Pension Alcázar** enroute from the cathedral. The rooms are fine (most with air conditioning) and the top floor rooms have ceiling fans but a fine large terrace (moderate, Dean Miranda 12, tel. 422-8457).

Hotel Simón (moderate-expensive, with four inexpensive singles, one block west of Ave. de la Constitución and the cathedral at Calle García de Vinuesa 19, tel. 422-6660, fax 456-2241, English spoken) in what was a private mansion typical of the eighteenth century, between my favorite tapas street and the cathedral, with an elegant courtyard and a good restaurant, is the best accommodations value I found, so reserve ahead. Nowhere near as good a value but a reasonable ace-in-the-hole is the nearby **Hotel Europa** (expensive, Calle Jimios 5, tel. 421-4305).

Eating in Sevilla

For tapas, barhop in these three areas: the Barrio de Santa Cruz is trendy, touristic, more expensive, but *muy romantico*. Walk from the cathedral up Mateos Gago a few blocks and melt into the narrow lanes on your right. You're very likely to enjoy some live music. The **Cervecería Giralda** and **Bodega Santa Cruz** are good places to start.

Across from the cathedral, west of Ave. de la Constitución is my favorite area to eat—follow Almirantazgo and Calle Arfe. Duck into the Plaza Cabildo (archway #19 off Arfe) for a bit of peace and maybe a splurge dinner at **Restaurant Figón del Cabildo**. **Calle Arfe** and the nearby streets are lined with colorful bars and no tourists, drop into the **Meson Sevilla** for chic tapas.

In the Triana District (cross the river at Puente San Telmo and walk to Puente Isabel II), you'll find classy bars (and restaurants) lining Calle Betis along the river. If you're looking for a fight, pop into the workingman's places one block in and say something derogatory about a local matador. **La Taberna** (a half-block back, between the two bridges, next to the police station) is cheap, youthful, and lively after 23:00. On the south end of Puente Isabel II, the bar in the yellow clock tower, Restaurant Maria Angeles, is spectacularly decorated, with a roof garden and great views of the river and old town. Many other good bars are nearby, especially **Kiosko Las Flores**.

For a non-tapas meal, there are plenty of atmospheric but touristy places in the cathedral/Santa Cruz area. The cheapest places line Alvarez Quintero, a street running north from the cathedral. For dinner you can splurge at the **Río Grande** restaurant across the river (turn right after crossing Puente San Telmo) with its shady deck over the river—good view, good food, and good service, open 20:00. Or eat the same thing—with the same view but fewer tablecloths—next door at the self-service **El Puerto** for one-third the price.

There is a covered fish-and-produce market with a small café/bar inside near the bullring (Pastor y Landero).

DAY 15

ANDALUSIA'S ROUTE OF THE WHITE VILLAGES

Today is small Andalusian hill town day. Leave Sevilla early and wind through the golden hills of the "Ruta de Pueblos Blancos" in search of the most exotic whitewashed villages. After several short stops, set up in Arcos de la Frontera.

Suggested Schedule—By Car	
8:00	Breakfast and depart.
9:30	Zahara.
11:00	Drive to Grazalema.
12:30	Lunch and wander in Grazalema.
15:00	Drive to Arcos de la Frontera (park at Parador).
16:00	Set up in hotel, climb the bell tower(s), explore the town, have dinner at the convent.

The Route

The remote hill towns of Andalusia are a joy to tour by car with Michelin map 446. Drivers can zip south on N-IV from Sevilla along the river following signs to Cádiz. Take the fast toll freeway (blue signs, E5, A4, 30 minutes, 830 ptas) or stick with the perfectly good and free N-IV. About halfway to Jerez, at Las Cabezas, take C343 to Villamartin. From there, circle scenically (and clockwise) through the thick of the Pueblos Blancos—Zahara and Grazalema to Arcos.

It's about 2 hours from Sevilla to Zahara. You'll find decent but very winding roads and sparse traffic. You'll wonder why they cut the road so long on the way in to Zahara. And then it gets worse if you take the tortuous series of switchbacks over the 4,500-foot summit of Puerto de Las Palomas on the direct but difficult road from Zahara to Grazalema. Remember to refer to your *Ruta de Pueblos Blancos* pamphlet.

Traffic flows through old Arcos only from west to east (coming from the east, circle south under the town).

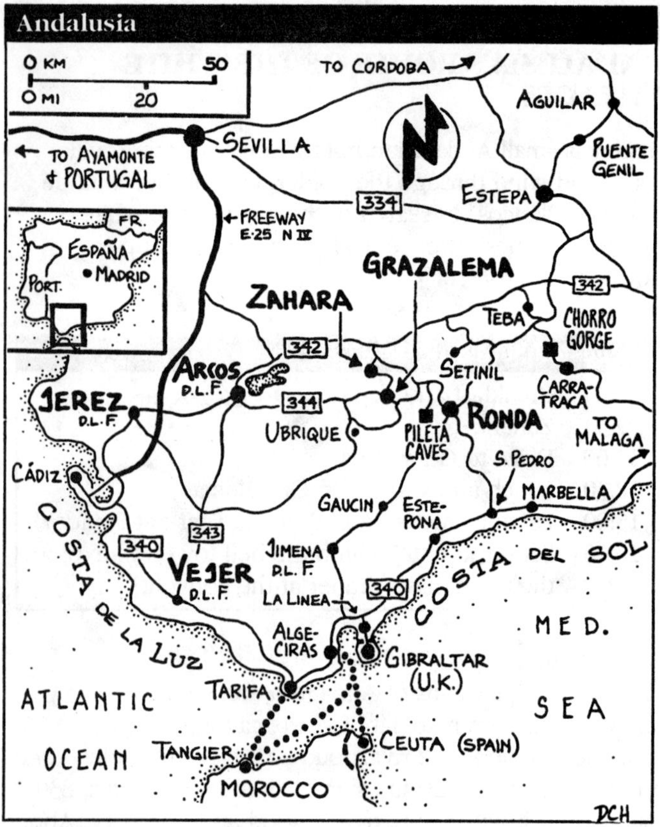

Turismo, most of my recommended hotels, and parking (Paseo Andalucia) are all in the west. Driving in Arcos is like threading needles. But if your car is small and the town seems quiet enough, follow signs to the Parador where you'll find the only old-town car park (cheap, maximum 2 hours, 9:30-14:00, 17:00-20:30, free on Saturday afternoons and all day Sunday).

By Bus and Train

Bus service to the Pueblos Blancos from Seville is limited, but workable. To explore the Pueblos Blancos well, rent a car in Seville and leave it in Granada or Algeciras. A few buses a day connect Seville and Arcos, one daily bus runs to Estepa, and there are several daily trips to Ronda. Arcos works well by bus with our itinerary.

Ronda is the only Pueblos Blancos town served by rail (transfer in Bobadilla). Train connections from Sevilla's Santa Justa station are very good: to Madrid, four a day, 8-10 hours (high-speed AVE train does the trip in 4 hours); to Córdoba, two a day, 4 hours; to Málaga, two a day, 3 hours. There is a *directo* to Granada (5 hours, leaving around 7:00).

Sightseeing Highlights—Andalusian Hill Towns

▲▲Zahara—This tiny town with a tingly setting under a Moorish castle (worth the climb) has a spectacular view. Zahara is a fine overnight stop for those who want to hear only the sounds of wind, birds, and elderly footsteps on ancient cobbles. The Hostal Marques de Zahara (inexpensive, San Juan 3, tel. 956/137261) and the homier Pensión Gonzalo next door (cheap, tel. 956/137217, the German-speaking daughter works at the Bar Vicente across the street) are fine values.

▲Grazalema—Another postcard-pretty hill town, Grazalema offers a royal balcony for a memorable picnic, a square where you can watch local old-timers playing cards, and plenty of quiet, whitewashed streets to explore. The town has several places that rent *camas* (rooms).

▲▲▲Arcos de la Frontera—Arcos, smothering its hilltop and tumbling down all sides like an oversized blanket, is larger than the other towns but equally atmospheric. The old center is a labyrinthine wonderland, a photographer's feast. Its spectacular location, on a pinnacle overlooking a vast Andalusian plain, is best appreciated from the tops of its two church bell towers.

You can climb each bell tower, passing through the tower-keeper's home. For a tip, he will give you a key and direct you skyward. The church farthest east, San Pedro, is most interesting. You'll probably meet Francisco Ramirez García, the church watchman who is also an *artesania de palma* (basket weaver). He'll show you his newspaper clippings, rummage through his fan mail, remind you "don't touch the bells," give you a teeny peep down at the church's nave, and send you up the tower. Climb to the bells and then on to the very top for the windy view (open whenever Sr. García wants). Brace your ears. Bring a picnic. The church interiors are also worth a look—open 11:00 to 13:00 and 17:00 to 19:30 in summer. Ask at the TI about free guided walking tours (in English at 11:30 and 18:00).

Much as it's trying, Arcos doesn't have much to offer other than its basic whitewashed self. The new English guidebook on Arcos, sold all over town, waxes long and poetic about very little. Since the churches are open only in the evenings and the town market is most interesting in the morning, and in-town parking is free overnight, you can arrive late and leave early. The bus stop is on the main road near the tourist office.

By the way, towns with "de la Frontera" in their names were established on the front line of the centuries-long fight to reconquer Spain from the Muslims, who were slowly pushed back into Africa.

Just below Arcos on the road to Ronda (C344) is a reservoir (Lago de Arcos). There's a bar in a pine forest with a great beach. A swim here is refreshing. For a more organized lake experience, there's the much-bragged-about "Mississippi paddle boat." What would Mark Twain say?

Sleeping in Arcos, telephone code 956, postal code: 11630.

Arcos is just being discovered, so it's weak on hotel and restaurant choices. There are only the "convent" and a very expensive parador in the old town. A cluster of room-and-board options can be found at the west end of town, a five-minute walk from the center (tourist office, open 9:00-14:00 and 17:00-18:30, Saturday 9:00-14:00, closed Sunday, tel. 956/702264, has Jerez maps).

Hotel Los Olivos (moderate-expensive, San Miguel 2, tel. 70 08 11, fax 70 20 18) is a bright, cool, and airy new place with a fine courtyard, roof garden, bar, view, friendly English-speaking folks, and easy parking. This is a poor man's parador—it's not cheap, but worth it, with a big American breakfast.

Hotel Restaurant "El Convento" (moderate, all with showers, Maldonado 2, tel. 70 23 33) deep in the old town just beyond the parador, is the best deal in town, cozier and cheaper than Los Olivos. Run by a hardworking family, several of its ten rooms have incredible view balconies. See restaurant listing below.

Parador de Arcos de la Frontera (11,500 ptas, more with a terrace, Plaza de España, tel. 70 05 00, fax 70 11 16) is royally located and, for all its elegance, reasonably priced. If you're going to experience a parador (and you can't get into the convent), this might be the one.

Fonda del Comércio (cheap, Debajo del Corral, at the west end of town near Turismo, tel. 70 00 57) is big, old, and barely acceptable, with saggy beds and no water in the rooms.

Two middle-range places, just outside town on the road to Ronda, are **Hostal Málaga** (inexpensive, Ave. Ponce de León 1, tel. 70 20 10) and **Hostal Voy-Voy** (inexpensive, Ave. Ponce de León 9, tel. 70 14 12).

Eating in Arcos

The parador is very expensive, though a costly drink on its million-dollar view terrace can be rationalized. The **Restaurante El Convento** (near the parador) has a wonderful atmosphere. The gracious lady who runs it is María Moreno Moreno (reminds me of Olive Oyl; her husband, Sr. Roldan, even faintly resembles Popeye; and the English-speaking daughter, Raquel, is just plain very likable). The food is good but not cheap. The 2,500 pta menu of the day could feed two and is the best value, including a fine red house wine and special local circular bread sticks (*picas de Arcos*).

The **Café Bar El Faro** (Debajo del Corral 16) is also good. Taste the great tapas at the typical **Alcaravan** in a cave near the Turismo. The best deal in Spain may be at the roadside diner with the green dinosaur in Venta de los Rios, 15 minutes from Arcos toward Vejer.

Other Andalusian Sightseeing Highlights
There are plenty of undiscovered and interesting hill towns to explore. I found that about half the towns I visited were worth remembering. Unfortunately, good information on the area is rare. The green Michelin guide skips the region entirely. A good map, the tourist brochure, and a spirit of adventure work fine. Here are some of my favorite finds for those with more time:

Estepa—Estepa, while getting popular with Spaniards who come here for the famous "Christmas Cakes," is still off the tourist circuit. The town hugs a small hill halfway between Córdoba and Málaga. Its crown is the convent of Santa Clara (1598), worth five stars in any guidebook but found in none. Enjoy the territorial view from the summit, then step into the quiet spiritual perfection of this little-known convent. Just sit in the chapel all alone and feel the beauty soak through your body.

Evening is prime time in Estepa—or any Andalusian town. The promenade, or *paseo*, begins as everyone gravitates to the central square. Estepa's spotless streets are shined nightly by the feet of ice-cream-licking strollers. The whole town strolls—it's like "cruising" without cars. Buy an "ice cream bocadillo" and follow suit. (Driving: Sevilla to Estepa, 2 hours on N334; Estepa to Ronda, 2 hours on N334, N342 to Campillos, and C341 into Ronda.)

Reasonable rooms in Estepa are on Avda. Andalucía: **Hostal El Quijote** (tel. 95/482-0965), and **Hostal Rico** (tel. 95/482-0866). Turismo tel. 95/482/1000.

Ortegicar—This teeny, six-horse, ten-dog complex of buildings around a castle keep is located a half mile off C341 on a dirt road, 7 miles north of Cuevas del Becerro on the way to Ronda. The nearest train station is La Ronda, 7 miles away. Hitch from there.

South of Estepa are the hill-capping village of Teba and the interesting towns of Manzanares and Carratraca. Skip the Chorro Gorge. It's not worth the drive unless you're a real gorgeophile.

Ronda
Ronda is the capital of the "white towns." With 40,000 people, it's one of the largest and, since it's within easy

day-trip range of the "Costa del Turismo," Ronda can be very crowded during the daytime. Still, it has the charm, history, bus and train connections, and nighttime magic to make it a good stop.

Ronda's main attractions are the gorge it straddles, the oldest bullring in Spain, and an interesting old town. The breathtaking ravine divides the town's labyrinthine Roman/Moorish quarter and its new, noisier, and more sprawling Mercadillo quarter. A graceful eighteenth-century bridge connects the two halves. Most things of touristic importance are clustered within a few blocks of this bridge—the bullring, view, tourist office, post office, and hotels. Beware—streets tend to change names with frustrating regularity. The best public parking lot is behind the bullring (100 ptas for 90 minutes).

The train station is 15 minutes by foot from the bridge in the new town (walk straight out and turn right on the main road). From the bus station (10 minutes away), walk downhill past the roundabout and keep going to reach the center.

The extremely helpful but busy tourist office is on the square opposite the bridge (open Monday-Friday 10:00-14:30 and sometimes 17:00-19:00, tel. 87 12 72). Helena Wirtanen works there and offers excellent daytrip excursions into the beautiful countryside around Ronda (tel. 287 55 56). Train information: 287-1662, buses: 287-2657. Bullfights are scheduled the first two weeks of September.

Sleeping and Eating in Ronda, telephone code: 95, postal code: 29400.

Ronda is full of reasonably priced, good-value accommodations, but is most crowded from mid-March through May and August through September. June and July are not bad. Off-season is from November through mid-March. Except for the first and last listings, all of my recommendations are a few minutes to left of the main square if you're facing the bridge.

Huespeudes La Española (cheap, José Aparicio 3, tel. 287 10 52) has a perfect location just off Plaza España around the corner from the tourist office. Its balcony, with a view of the peaceful sunset on the mountains, makes it very popular.

The friendly **Huéspedes Atienza** (cheap, Calvo Asencio 3, tel. 287 52 36) is in a great paseo part of the new town, 4 minutes from the bridge. (note: C. Cristo turns into Calvo Asencio).

Hostal Ronda Sol (inexpensive, Almendra 11, tel. 287 44 97) is less central but has a homey atmosphere and is a fine value. The next-door **Hostal Biarritz** offers a similarly good value (7 Alemandra, tel. 287-2910). The **Hostal Virgin del Rocio** is spotless and very central (inexpensive, C. Nueva 18, tel. 287 74 25)

Ronda offers two good splurges. The new and impressive **Don Miguel** is right on the gorge, just left of the bridge. Many rooms have gorge-ous views and stunning balconies (moderate-expensive, C. Villanueva 8, tel. 287 77 22, fax 287 83 77). The royal **Reina Victoria** (expensive, Jerez 25, tel. 287 12 40, fax 287 10 75), hanging over the gorge at the edge of town, has a great view—Hemingway loved it—but you'll pay for it.

When choosing a place to eat, dodge the tourist traps. One block across the main street from the bullring, the Plaza del Socorro has plenty of cheap tapa bars and restaurants. **Las Cañas** at Duque de la Victoria 2 on the corner of the plaza is small, simple, and serves good food. The **Restaurante Alhambra** (Pedro Romero 9) serves a fine and reasonable three-course dinner (their mussels and mousse are excellent). The best view drink in town is had at the outdoor terrace of the Don Miguel hotel, at the bridge.

Pileta Caves, near Ronda

The Cuevas de la Pileta are about the best look a tourist can get at prehistoric cave painting these days. The caves, complete with stalagmites, bones, and 25,000-year-old paintings, are 17 miles from Ronda. By car, go north on C339, exit toward Benoajan, then follow the signs, bearing right just before Benoajan, up to the dramatic dead-end. Or take the train to Benoajan (tricky scheduling, get help in Ronda's station) and hike 2 hours uphill to the caves.

The farmer who lives down the hill leads groups through from 9:00 to 14:00 and 16:00 to 19:00 (500 ptas, leave nothing of value in the car). His grandfather discovered the caves. He is a master at hurdling the language barrier and, as you walk the cool kilometer, he'll spend over an hour pointing out lots of black and red drawings (five times as old as the Egyptian pyramids) and some weirdly recognizable natural formations like the Michelin man and a Christmas tree. The famous caves at Altamira are closed, so if you want to see Neolithic paintings in Spain, this is it.

Córdoba—This is a world-class city and a center of Moorish civilization in Spain. But I've left it out, thinking that on a short trip, seeing two of the three Moorish and Andalusian biggies (Granada, Sevilla, and Córdoba) is enough. And I like the others better. Still, Córdoba has lots of historic importance, some unique Moorish architecture, and it's well-connected by train and freeway with the rest of Andalusia.

DAY 16

ARCOS DE LA FRONTERA, JEREZ, TARIFA

Today you get your last dose of Andalusian hill life before taking the short drive to Jerez to sample the city's smooth horses and smoother sherry. Then on to the least-developed piece of Spain's generally overdeveloped south coast—the whitewashed port (and windsurfing haven) of Tarifa.

Suggested Schedule—By Car	
9:00	After a quick early morning stroll through Arcos, get to Jerez in time for a 10:00 sherry *bodega* tour and a noon look at her famous horses.
14:00	Drive south, with possible stops in Medina Sidonia and Vejer, or go straight to Tarifa for some beach time.
16:00	Arrive in Tarifa. Book tomorrow's tour to Morocco, explore the bleached old town.

The Route: Arcos to Tarifa (80 miles)

The drive from Arcos to Jerez is a zippy 30 minutes. Then follow signs to Medina Sidonia south on the small road less traveled, on to Vejer, and from there to Tarifa. A great freeway connects Sevilla and Jerez de la Frontera.

By Bus and Train

Those traveling by train will have to convert to bus to see this isolated corner of Spain. Verify bus schedules at the Arcos Tursimo. While I'd take one of the few daily direct buses from Arcos to Ronda (passing through the heart of the beautiful Pueblos Blancos region) and skip Jerez and Tarifa, this day is feasible by bus. Very frequent bus service connects Arcos and Jerez (40-minute ride) and Jerez and Cádiz (1-hour ride). Less frequent service (about eight trips per day) connect Cádiz and Tarifa in 2 hours. A few daily trips run straight from Arcos to Cádiz. The closest and most useful train station is in Jerez with frequent service to Cádiz and Seville.

Sightseeing Highlights—Jerez to Tarifa

Jerez, with nearly 200,000 people, is your typical big-city mix of industry, garbage, car bandits, and dusty concrete suburbs, but it has two popular claims to touristic fame—horses and sherry. (Turismo tel. 956/33 11 50. Telephone code: 956)

▲▲Sherry *bodega* tour—Spain produces over 10 million gallons per year of this fortified wine ranging in taste from *fine* (dry) to *amontillado* (medium) to *dulce* (sweet). The name "sherry" comes from attempts by an Englishman to pronounce Jerez. Your tourist map of Jerez (pick up at Sevilla or Arcos Turismo) is speckled with wine glasses. Each of these is a sherry *bodega* (cellar) that offers tours and tasting. Most places welcome individuals without reservations Monday through Friday from 9:30 to 12:30 (closed in August), giving 20- to 30-minute tours in English for free or a nominal charge. The highlight of each tour is the tasting session at the end.

Bodegas giving tours are Harveys of Bristol (C. Arcos 53, tel. 15 10 30), Gonzalez Byas (Manuel María Gonzalez 12, tel. 34 00 00), and Williams and Humbert (Nuño de Caña, near the TI and horse show, tel. 33 13 00). Always call first to check the English tour times.

▲▲The Royal Andalusian School of Equestrian Art—If you're into horses, this is a must. Even if you're not, this is horse art like you've never seen. The school does its "How the Andalusian Horses Dance" show each Thursday at noon (1,500 ptas). This is an equestrian ballet put together with choreography taken from classical dressage movements, purely Spanish music, and costumes from the nineteenth century. The stern horsemen and their obedient horses prance, jump, and do-si-do in time to the music, to the delight of an arena filled with mostly local horse aficionados. Training sessions are open to the public on Monday, Tuesday, Wednesday, and Friday from 11:00 to 13:00, offering (to my untrained eye) an almost equally impressive show for one-fourth the price. You can sip sherry in the arena's bar to complete the sherry experience. Follow signs from the center of Jerez (to Real Escuela Andaluza de Arte Ecuestre) to the guarded parking lot. For reservations, call 956/31 11 11.

Medina Sidonia—This place has no Turismo (read "no tourists"). It is white as can be surrounding its church-and-castle ruin-topped hill. Give it a quick look as you drive south. Signs to Vejar will route you through the middle to Plaza de España—great for a coffee stop. You can drive from here up to the church (Plazuela de la Yglesia Mayor) where, for a tip, the man will show you around. Even without a tip you can climb yet another belfry for yet another vast Andalusian view. The castle ruins aren't worth the trouble.

▲▲Vejer de la Frontera—Okay, one more whitewashed hill town. Vejer, just 20 miles north of Tarifa, will lure all but the very jaded off the highway. Vejer's strong Moorish roots give it a distinct Moroccan (or Greek island) flavor—you know, black-clad women whitewashing their homes, and lanes that can't decide if they are roads or stairways. Only a few years ago women wore veils. The town has no real sights (other than its women's faces), no Turismo, and very little tourism, but makes for a pleasant stop.

A newcomer on Andalusia's tourist map, the old town of Vejer has only two hotels. The Convento de San Francisco (expensive, but bargain-able in off-season, tel. 956/45 10 01, fax 45 10 04, English spoken) is a poor man's parador in a classy refurbished convent. They have the rare but unnecessary Vejer town map. A much better value is the clean and charming Hostal La Posada (inexpensive, Los Rededios 21, tel. 956/45 02 58, or 45 01 11). Both are at the entrance to the old town, at the top of the switchbacks by the town's lone traffic cop.

The coast near Vejer is lonely, with fine but windswept beaches. It's popular with windsurfers and sand flies. The Battle of Trafalgar was fought just off Cabo de Trafalgar (a nondescript lighthouse today). I drove the circle so that you who buy this book need not.

Tarifa

This most southerly city in all of Europe is a pleasant alternative to gritty, noisy Algeciras. It's an Arabic-looking town with a lovely beach, an old castle, restaurants swimming in fresh seafood, inexpensive places to sleep, enough windsurfers to sink a ship, and best of all, hassle-free boats to Morocco.

As I stood on the town promenade under the castle, looking out at almost-touchable Morocco across the Strait of Gibraltar, I regretted only that I didn't have this book to steer me clear of wretched Algeciras on earlier trips. Tarifa, with daily 1-hour hydrofoil trips to Tangiers, is the best jumping-off point for a Moroccan side trip.

Tarifa has no blockbuster sights. Its so-so castle, named after Guzmán el Bueno (a general who gained fame by proudly refusing to negotiate with his enemies as they killed his son), is surrounded by cool lanes and white-washed houses. Don't miss the view-point patio near the castle. Tarifa's main harbor activity seems to be the daily coming and going of the boat to Tangiers. A few minutes from downtown is a pleasant sheltered beach, Playa Chica, and just beyond that beach is a wild and desolate stretch of pristine shoreline, the Playa de Lances.

Lately, the town's character has changed (to many, suffered) as it has become famous as Europe's windsurfing paradise. With VW vans stacked high with windsurf gear, lines of wind-blown beach huts, German menus, T-shirts, and thongs, Tarifa has become more of a busy resort. Telephone code: 956.

Orientation: The tourist office is in a street-side booth, a block from the first hotel listing on Avda. de Andalucía, tel. 68 41 86. Pick up a town map and the photocopied walking tour. Get your boat ticket as soon as possible since there is only one a day and they do sell out. Prices are the same at all offices, so you might call ahead or stop by the roadside agency you'll see as you drive into town (Marruecotur, highway 340, km 82, Batalla del Salado 57, tel. 58 40 75 or 68 40 01).

Sleeping and Eating in Tarifa, telephone code: 956, postal code: 11380.
These accommodations are listed in the order you'll pass them arriving from Vejer, Cádiz or Sevilla. The first four listings are better for drivers, right off the main drag (the Batalla del Salado), with easy parking, in the modern, ugly part of town. You'll walk past them by turning right out of the bus station ticket office and heading toward the old city center. The last four are in or bordering the old town, very quiet and far from the windsurfing safari. Room rates vary with the season, sometimes doubling from low to high season. August is very crowded, but prices are at their highest from July through September. October through December is mid-season, and January through May is low season.

Hotel La Mirada (inexpensive-moderate, Calle San Sebastián 48, tel. 68 44 27, fax 68 11 12), is 2 blocks to the right of the main drag, about 5 blocks from the old town. It's new and has some sea-view rooms.

The motel-style **Hostal Tarik** (inexpensive, Calle San Sebastián 32, tel. 68 52 40) is 1 block toward the town center from La Mirada and surrounded by warehouses.

Hostal Alborada (inexpensive-moderate, Calle San José 52, tel. 64 11 40, fax 68 19 35) is another squeaky-clean place with a pleasant courtyard. It's a couple of blocks closer to the old town on an ugly street.

The cheery, family-run **Hostal Avenida** (inexpensive, Calle Pío XII, just off the main drag, tel. 68 48 18) is clean and comfy but on a busy street leading into town.

Fonda Villanueva (cheap, Avda. de Andalucía 11, tel. 68 41 49, just to the right of the old town gate next to the Turismo booth) is your best budget bet; friendly, though no English is spoken, and with a great terrace overlooking the old town.

The following listings can all be reached by entering the gate into the old city. **Hostal la Calzada** (inexpensive, C. Justino Pertinez 7, tel. 68 43 46; veer left and down from the gate) has eight well-appointed, quiet, bright, and airy rooms right in the noisy-at-night old-town thick of things. If you get to the cathedral, it's 1 block to the right up the small alley. Just above the Hostal la Calzada (you may pass it enroute to the Hostal La Calzada) is the bare-bones and funky **La Casa Concha Pensión** (cheap, San Rosendo 4, tel. 68 49 31).

The new **Hostal Alameda** (inexpensive-moderate, Paseo Alameda 4, tel. 68 11 81; veer right upon entering the old gate and go all the way down) glistens in happy pastels, overlooking a square where the local children play, on the edge of the old town near the port. It has 11 rooms above its restaurant and the prettiest business card in all of Spain.

The **Chan Bar Restaurant** on the main drag, Batalla del Salado, about 5 blocks north of the recommended hotels in the new town, serves a fine, cheap menu. You'll find good tapas throughout the old town and good seafood in places around Plaza San Mateo.

DAY 17

A DAY IN MOROCCO

And now for something completely different, plunge into Africa for a day. As you step off the boat you realize that the hour-long crossing provided more of a cultural change than flying all the way from home to Iberia did. Morocco needs no museums; the sights are living in the streets. The one-day excursions (daily except Sunday) from Tarifa are well-organized and reliable, and given the steep price of the boat passage alone, the tour package is a good value for those who can spare only a day for Morocco.

Suggested Schedule	
9:30	All aboard!
11:00	Arrive in Tangiers, meet bus and guide, tour city, lunch, see countryside, shop, and sail Strait of Gibraltar back home.
19:00	Relax back in Tarifa.

Morocco in a Day?

There are many ways to experience Morocco, and a day in Tangiers is probably the worst. But if all you have is a day, this is a real and worthwhile adventure. Tangiers is the Tijuana of Morocco, and everyone there seems to be expecting you.

For just a day, I'd recommend the tours organized in Tarifa. For 7,000 ptas you get a round-trip hydrofoil crossing; a good guide to meet you at the harbor and hustle you through the hustlers and onto your bus; a bus tour of the area's highlights—ritzy neighborhoods, city tour, trip to the desolate Atlantic Coast for some impressively rugged African scenery, and the famous ride-a-camel stop—a walk through the *medina* (market) area of Tangiers with a too-thorough look at a carpet shop; a chance to do battle with the sales-starved local merchants; and a great lunch in a palatial Moroccan setting with belly dance entertainment.

Morocco

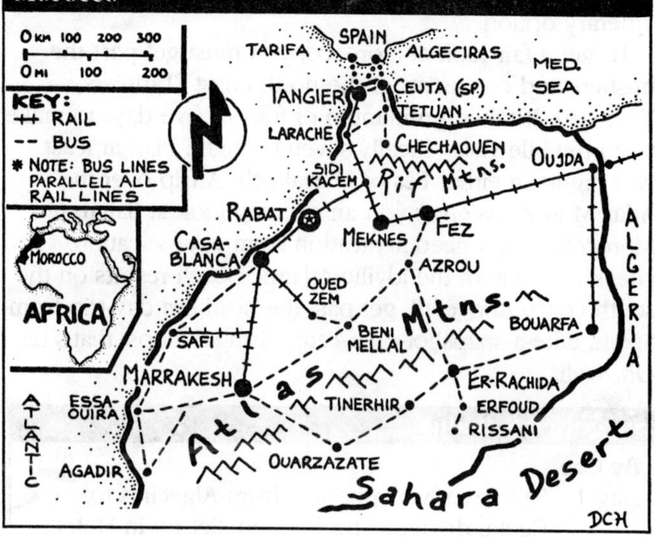

Sound cheesy? Maybe, but no amount of packaging can gloss over how exotic and different this culture really is. This kind of cultural voyeurism is almost embarrassing, but it is nonstop action and more memorable than another day in Spain. The shopping is . . . Moroccan. Bargain hard!

The day trip is so tightly organized you'll have hardly any time alone in Tangiers. For many people, that's just fine. Some, however, spend a night in Tangiers and return the next day. Ask about the two-day 12,000-pta tour at the tourist office in Tarifa. (Tarifa travel agencies: Marruecotur, tel. 58 40 75, and Tourafrica at the boat dock, tel. 68 47 51.)

Itinerary Option: An Extended Tour of Morocco

While the hour-long cruise to Tangiers from southern Spain takes you farther culturally than did the trip all the way from the U.S.A. to Spain, you really should seriously consider going deeper into the interior. Morocco is incredibly rich in cultural thrills per mile, minute, and dollar—but you'll pay a price in hassles and headaches. It's a package deal and, if danger's your business, it's a great itinerary option.

To get a fair look at Morocco, you must get past the hustlers and con artists of the north coast (Tangiers, Tétouan). It takes a minimum of four or five days to make a worthwhile visit—ideally seven or eight. Plan at least two nights in either Fès or Marrakech. A trip over the Atlas Mountains gives you an exciting look at Saharan Morocco. If you need a vacation from your vacation, check into one of the idyllic Atlantic beach resorts on the south coast. Above all, get past the northern day-trip-from-Spain, take-a-snapshot-on-a-camel fringe. Oops, that's us. Oh, well.

Suggested Schedule

By Car

Day 1	Sail as early as possible from Algeciras to Ceuta, drive to Chechaouen. Set up in Hotel Chaouen on main square facing the old town.
Day 2	Drive to Fès. Find hotel. Take orientation tour.
Day 3	Free to explore the Fès medina. Evening: classy dinner and cultural show.
Day 4	Drive to Volubilis near Meknès. Tour ancient Roman ruins, possibly stop in cities of Moulay Idriss and Meknès. Drive back to Chechaouen. Same hotel, possibly reserved from Day 1.
Day 5	Return to Spain.

By Train and Bus

Day 1	Sail as early as possible from Algeciras to Tangiers. Take the 4-hour train or bus ride to Rabat (Hotel Splendide).
Day 2	Sightsee in Rabat—Salé, King's Palace, royal tomb.
Day 3	Take the train to Casablanca (nothing to stop for), catch the Marrakech Express from there to the "red city." Get set up near the medina in Marrakech.
Day 4	Free in Marrakech.
Day 5	Free in Marrakech. Night train back to Rabat.
Day 6	Return to Spain.

Orientation (Mental)

Thrills: Morocco *is* culture shock. It makes Spain and Portugal look meek and mild. You'll encounter oppressive friendliness, the Arabic language, squiggly writing, the Islamic faith, and ancient cities; it is a photographer's delight, very cheap, with plenty of hotels, surprisingly easy transportation, and a variety of terrain from Swiss-like mountain resorts to fairy-tale mud-brick oasis towns to luxuriously natural beaches to bustling desert markets.

Spills: Morocco *is* culture shock. Many are overwhelmed by its intensity, poverty, aggressive beggars, brutal heat, and slick con men. Most visitors have some intestinal problems (the big "D"). Most women are harassed on the streets by horny, but generally harmless, men. Things don't work smoothly. In fact, compared to Morocco, Spain resembles Sweden for efficiency. The language barrier is a problem since French, not English, is Morocco's second language, and most English-speaking Moroccans the tourist meets are hustlers. This is Islam. People don't see the world through the same filters we do, and some very good parents proudly name their sons Saddam.

Leave aggressive itineraries and split-second timing for Germany. Morocco must be taken on its own terms. In Morocco things go smoothly only *"In Sha Allah"*—if God so wills.

Spain to Morocco Options

Tarifa-Tangiers (6,000 ptas round-trip, 1-hour crossing, 10:00 daily except Sunday, passengers only; day-tour option including lunch and guided bus tour is 7,000 ptas, only 1,200 more; two days with hotel and meals included for 12,000 ptas).

Algeciras-Ceuta (1,700 ptas each way, 2-hour crossing, three or more a day, 7,000 ptas for a car). Ceuta is a not very interesting Spanish possession in North Africa. You'll cross from there into Morocco. It's the best car-entry point but not for those relying on public transport.

Algeciras-Tangiers (3,500 ptas each way, 3-hour crossing, at least six crossings a day, 9,000 ptas for a car).

Reservations are a good idea for the Tarifa trips since tour groups can book up the once-a-day departure. No visa or shots are necessary; just bring your passport. If possible, buy a round-trip ticket from Spain. I've had departures from Morocco delayed by ticket-buying hassles there. Prices are uniform in the many travel agencies advertising trips to Morocco.

Change money on arrival only at a bank. Banks have uniform rates. The black market is dangerous. Change only what you need and keep the bank receipt to reconvert if necessary. Don't leave the country with Moroccan money.

If you're driving a car, sail to Ceuta, a Spanish possession. Crossing the border is a bit unnerving, since you'll be hustled through several bureaucratic hoops. You'll go through customs, buy Moroccan insurance for your car (cheap and easy), and really feel at the mercy of a bristly bunch of shady-looking people you'd rather not be at the mercy of. Most cars are shepherded through by a guy who will expect a tip. Relax, let him grease those customs wheels. He's worth it. As soon as possible, hit the road and drive to Chechaouen, the best first stop for those driving.

If you're relying on public transportation, you should sail to Tangiers, blast your way through customs, listen to no hustler who tells you there's no way out until tomorrow, and walk from the boat dock over to the train station. From there, just set your sights on Rabat, a dignified European-type town with fewer hustlers, and make it your get-acquainted stop in Morocco. From Rabat, trains will take you farther south.

Moroccan trains are quite good. Second class is cheap and comfortable. There are only two lines: Oujda-Fès-Meknès-Rabat-Casablanca (seven trains daily) and Tangiers-Rabat-Casablanca-Marrakech (three trains daily).

Sightseeing Highlights—Moroccan Towns

▲▲Chechaouen—Just 2 hours by bus or car from Tétouan, this is the first pleasant town beyond the Tijuana-type north coast. Mondays and Thursdays are colorful market days. Stay in the classy old Hotel Chaouen on Plaza el-Makhzen. This former Spanish parador faces the old town and offers fine meals and a pleasant refuge from hustlers. Wander deep into the whitewashed old town from here.

▲▲▲Marrakech—Morocco's gateway to the south, this market city is a constant folk festival bustling with djelaba-clad Berber tribespeople, a colorful center where the desert, mountain, and coastal regions merge.

The new city has the train station, and the main boulevard (Mohammed V) is lined with banks, airline offices, a post office, a tourist office, and the city's most comfortable hotels.

The old city features the mazelike medina and the huge Djemaa el-Fna, a square seething with people, usually resembling a 43-ring Moroccan circus. Near this square you'll find hordes of hustlers, plenty of eateries, and cheap hotels (to check for bugs, step into the dark hotel room, then flip on the lights, and count 'em as they flee).

▲▲▲Fès—More than just a funny hat that tipsy Shriners wear, Fès is the religious and artistic center of Morocco. It bustles with craftsmen, pilgrims, shoppers, and shops. Like most large Moroccan cities, it has a distinct new town (*ville nouvelle*) from the French colonial period and a more exotic—and stressful—old Arabic town where you'll find the medina. The Fès marketplace is Morocco's best.

▲▲Rabat—Morocco's capital and most European city, Rabat is the most comfortable and least stressful place to start your North African experience. You'll find a colorful market (in the old neighboring town of Salé), several great bits of Islamic architecture (mausoleum of Mohammed V), the king's palace, mellow hustlers, and comfortable hotels (try Hótel Splendide, the Peace Corps' favorite, at 2 rue Ghazzah, near where Ave. Mohammed V hits the medina, tel. 07/23283).

Extend your Moroccan trip three or four days with an excursion south over the Atlas Mountains. Buses go from Marrakech to Ouarzazate (short stop), then to Tinerhir (great oasis town, comfy hotel, overnight stop). Next day, go to Er Rachidia (formerly Ksar es Souk) and take the overnight bus to Fès.

By car, drive from Fès south, staying in the small mountain town of Ifrane, and then continue deep into the desert country past Er Rachidia and on to Rissani (market days, Sunday, Tuesday, and Thursday). From there, you can explore nearby mud-brick towns still living in the Middle Ages. Hire a guide to drive you past where the road stops, cross-country to an oasis village (Merzouga) where you can climb a sand dune to watch the sun rise over the vastness of Africa. Only a sea of sand separates you from Timbuktu.

Helpful Hints

Friday is the Muslim day of rest when most of the country closes down.

In Morocco, marijuana (*kif*) is as illegal as it is popular, as many Americans in local jails would love to remind you. Some dealers who sell it cheap make their profit after you get arrested. Cars and buses are stopped and checked by police routinely throughout Morocco—especially in the north and in the Chechaouen region, Morocco's kif capital.

Bring good information with you from home or Spain. The *Let's Go: Spain, Portugal and Morocco* book is indispensable. The *Real Guide to Morocco* is also excellent as is the green *Michelin Morocco* guidebook (if you read French). Buy the best map you can find locally—names are always changing, and it's helpful to have towns, roads, and place-names written in Arabic.

If you're driving, never rely on the oncoming driver's skill. Drive very defensively. Night driving is dangerous. Your U.S. license is all you need. Pay a guard to watch your car overnight.

While Moroccans are some of Africa's wealthiest people, you are still incredibly rich to them. This imbalance causes predictable problems. Wear your money belt, don't be a sucker to clever local con artists, and haggle when appropriate (prices skyrocket for tourists).

You'll attract hustlers—and I don't mean Paul Newman—like flies at every famous tourist sight. They'll lie to you, get you lost, blackmail you, and pester the heck out of you. Never leave your car or baggage where you can't get back to it without your "guide." Anything you buy in their company gets them a 20 to 30 percent commission. Normally, locals, shopkeepers, and police will come to your rescue when the hustler's heat becomes unbearable. I usually hire a young kid as a guide, since it's helpful to have a translator and once you're "taken" the rest seem to leave you alone.

Navigate the labyrinthine medinas by altitude, gates, and famous mosques, towers, or buildings. Write down what gate you came in so you can enjoy being lost—temporarily. *Souk* is Arabic for a particular "department" (such as leather, yarn, or metal work) of the medina.

Health

Morocco is much more hazardous to your health than Spain or Portugal. Eat in clean, not cheap, places. Peel fruit, eat only cooked vegetables, and drink reliably bottled water (Sidi Harazem or Sidi Ali). When you do get diarrhea—and you should plan on it—adjust your diet (small and bland, no milk or grease) or fast for a day, but make sure you replenish lost fluids. Relax; most diarrhea is not exotic or serious, just an adjustment that will run its course.

Language

The Arabic squiggle-script, its many difficult sounds, and the fact that French is Morocco's second language, make communication tricky for us English-speaking monoglots.

A little French will go a long way, but do learn a few words in Arabic. Have your first local friend teach you "thank you," "excuse me," "yes," "no," "okay," "hello," "good-bye," "how are you," and how to count to ten. Listen carefully and write the pronunciations down phonetically. Bring an Arabic phrase book.

Make a point of learning the local number symbols; they are not like ours (which we call "Arabic"). Car license plates use both kinds of numbers—great for practicing on. *La* means no. In markets, I sing "la la la la la" to my opponents. *La shokeron* (think "sugar on") means "No, thank you."

DAY 18

GIBRALTAR AND THE COSTA DEL SOL

After your day in Africa, a day in England may be your cup of tea. And that's just where you're going today—to the land of fish and chips, pubs and bobbies, pounds and pence—Gibraltar. Following this splash of uncharacteristically sunny England, enter the bikini-strangled land of basted bodies on the beach, the Costa del Sol. Bed down in this congested region's closest thing to pleasant, the happy town of Nerja, for a firsthand look at Europe's beachy playground.

Suggested Schedule—By Car	
8:00	Drive to Gibraltar, breakfast British-style. Morning in town, ride the lift to the Rock's summit, enjoy the view points. Fish and chips for lunch? Shop British at the Safeway next to the border crossing.
14:00	Drive the length of the very built-up Costa del Sol. Short stop in "Turistamolinos."
18:00	Arrive and set up in Nerja. Evening on the "balcony of Europe."

The Route: Tarifa to Nerja (150 miles)

The short and scenic drive from peaceful Tarifa past Algeciras to La Línea (the Spanish town bordering Gibraltar) takes 45 minutes. There's a scenic rest stop (with café) just outside Tarifa for great rock viewing. Upon arrival at the Gibraltar border, the resident con artist may tell you you can't drive into Gibraltar. The local police say otherwise. There is often a long line of cars at the border, and parking in Spain and walking in is an option. The border is actually an airstrip, and when the light is green look left, right, and up, then cross. Just before the airstrip is a big Safeway with a café and viewing terrace. Drop in for a blast of Britain and some fun culture shock, not to mention a good opportunity to satisfy your craving for any British edibles. From Gibraltar, the trip along the Costa del Sol is (barring traffic problems) smooth and easy by car. Just follow the coastal highway east. After Málaga, you'll follow signs to Almería and Motril.

By Bus and Train

From Tarifa, a series of bus connections starting with Algeciras (10 daily, a half-hour trip), then Algeciras to Málaga (10 per day, 6 hours), and finally from Málaga to Nerja (8 per day, 2 hours) will take you through the entire Costa del Sol and all day to reach Nerja. To Gibraltar, there are regular bus connections from Algeciras to La Línea. From La Línea, it's a 30-minute walk into downtown Gibraltar. You'll find plenty of aggressive cabbies at the border who'd love to give you a tour; for those with more money than time, this can be a fine value. Otherwise, small buses (cheap, twice an hour) shuttle visitors from the border into the center.

Good train destinations from Algeciras are Ronda, Málaga, Granada and Sevilla. All four rides are very scenic and the trip to Málaga (with bus connections to Nerja) via Bobadilla and El Choro is one of Spain's most scenic mountain train rides. The Algeciras train station is about 4 blocks directly inland from the ferry terminal on the far side of the tall Octavia Hotel (walk up C. Juan de Cierva).

Sightseeing Highlights—Spain's South Coast

▲▲▲The Rock and Town of Gibraltar—One of the last bits of the empire that the sun used to never set on, Gibraltar is a fun mix of Anglican properness, "God Save the Queen" tattoos, military memories, and tourist shops. The British soldiers you'll see are enjoying this cushy assignment in the Mediterranean sun as a reward for enduring and surviving an assignment in another remnant of the British Empire—Northern Ireland. While things are cheaper in pounds (and the exchange desk at Safeway charges no commission), your Spanish money works as well as your English words here.

The real highlight is the spectacular Rock itself. From the south end of Main Street, you can catch the cable car to the top with a stop at the Apes' Den on the way. From the "Top of the Rock" you can explore old ramparts and drool at the 360-degree view of Morocco, the Strait of Gibraltar, Algeciras and its bay, and the twinkling Costa del Sol arcing eastward. Below you stretches the giant water "catchment system" that the British built to catch rainwater in the not-so-distant past, when Spain allowed neither water nor tourists to cross its disputed border. The views are especially crisp on brisk off-season days. Buying a one-way ticket up saves a little money and gives you a chance to hike down—and maybe get a close encounter with one of the famous (and very jaded) "Apes of Gibraltar." Keep your distance from the apes and beware their kleptomaniac tendencies. On your way down, notice the WW II casements, or underground defenses, that Britain built into the Rock to secure its toehold on the Iberian peninsula. If you like military history, view the Gibraltar Laser Experience. Back in town you can tour the Gibraltar Museum on Bomb House Lane. The Tourist Offices are on Mackintosh Square (tel. 75555) and Cathedral Square (tel. 76400). Rooms in Gibraltar are not cheap. Telephone code: 010/350.

▲▲**Costa del Sol**—It's so bad, it's interesting. To Northern Europeans, the sun is a drug, and this is their needle. Anything resembling a quaint fishing village has been bikini-strangled and Nivea-creamed. Oblivious to the concrete, pollution, ridiculous prices, and traffic jams, tourists lie on the beach like mindless game hens on skewers—cooking, rolling, and sweating under their sun.

Where Europe's most popular beach isn't crowded by high-rise hotels, it's in a freeway chokehold. While wonderfully undeveloped beaches between Tarifa and Cádiz and east of Alveria are ignored, lemmings make the scene where the coastal waters are so polluted that hotels are required to provide swimming pools. It's a wonderful study in human nature.

For your Costa del Sol experience, consider a stop at the Aspen of beach resorts, Marbella, and its carbon monoxide-drenched sisters where Ronald McDonald laughs happily at the traffic jams, then consider spending

Costa del Sol

the afternoon and evening at one of the other resorts listed here.

Marbella—This is the most polished and posh of the Costa del Sol's resorts. Look for the Turismo sign to the right as you enter Marbella's center and park near here (Marbella is a stop on the Algeciras–Málaga bus route; to reach the center, turn left out of the bus station). Cross the main street at the signal closest to the Turismo and walk up to the old city's pedestrian section, veering right. While the high-priced boutiques, immaculate streets and beautifully landscaped squares are testimony to Marbella's arrival on the world-class-resort scene, cheap accommodations can still be found in old Marbella. Have a *cafe con leche* on the beautiful Plaza de Naranjas before wandering back down to new Marbella and the high rise beach-front apartment buildings. Check out Marbella's beautiful beach scene before leaving.

San Pedro de Alcantara—The relatively undeveloped sandy beach is popular with young travelers heading for Morocco (a good place to find a partner for a North African adventure). San Pedro's neighbor is Puerto Banus, "where the world casts anchor." This luxurious jet-set port, complete with casino, is a strange mix of Rolls-Royces, yuppies, boutiques, rich Arabs, and budget browsers.

Fuengirola/Torremolinos—The most built-up part of the region, where those most determined to be envied settle down, it's a bizarre world of Scandinavian package tours, flashing lights, pink flamenco, multilingual menus, and all-night happiness. Fuengirola is like a Spanish Mazatlán with a few less pretentious, older budget hotels between the main drag and the beach. The water here is clean enough (but too salty to drink) and the night life fun and easy. James Michener's idyllic Torremolinos is long gone—amazingly, plants have been sighted growing here.

Almuñecar—Smaller and the least touristy, where a fray of alleys in the old town and a salty fishing village atmosphere survive amid high-rise hotels.

Nerja

See Day 19.

DAY 19

COSTA DEL SOL TO GRANADA

After a beach-easy morning and lunch in Nerja, drop into the immense Nerja caves, then say "Adiós" to the Mediterranean as you head inland through the rugged Sierra Nevada mountains to the historic city of Granada. The last stronghold of the Moorish kingdom, Granada still has an exotically tangled Arab quarter and the lush Alhambra palace.

Suggested Schedule—By Car	
Morning	Free in town and on beach. Call to arrange or reconfirm Granada room.
14:00	Tour Nerja caves.
16:00	Drive to Granada.
18:00	Set up in Granada. Sunset from San Nicolas in Albaicín.
20:00	Dinner in Albaicín.

The Route: Nerja to Granada (80 miles, 90 minutes, 100 views)

Drive along the coast to Salobrena, catching E103 north for about 40 miles to Granada. While scenic side trips may beckon, don't arrive late in Granada without a firm reservation. In Granada, follow signs to the Alhambra and park (at least temporarily) on the Plaza Nueva or along Gomerez.

By Bus and Train

Skip the caves and take the 2-hour bus trip to Granada via a transfer in Motril (frequent service from Nerja to Motril and from Motril to Granada). There are a few direct trips to Granada, usually at inconvenient times. If you stay two nights in Nerja, consider the direct morning departure to Granada. Schedules are available at Nerja's Turismo. Neither the bus nor the train station is central in Granada, but bus #11, from near the cathedral, connects them. Taxis are cheap! Train information: 22 34 97. Bus information: 25 13 38.

Nerja

Somehow Nerja, while cashing in on the fun-in-the-sun culture, has actually kept much of its quiet Old World charm. It has several good beaches (the best is down the walkway to the right of the Restaurant Marisol just off the Balcon de Europa); a fun evening paseo, culminating in the proud "Balcony of Europe" terrace; enough nightlife; and locals who get more excited about their many festivals than the tourists do. Nerja's beach crowds thin as you walk farther from town. The Nerja tourist office (4 Puerta del Mar, tel. 252 15 31, open Monday-Friday 10:00-14:00 and 18:00-20:00, Saturday 10:00-13:00, closed Sunday) has town maps, tips on beaches and side trips, and Granada maps. For a taste of the British expatriate scene, drop in to W.H. Whiffs bookstore at C. Cristo 10 or tune in to Coastline Radio at 97.8.

Sleeping and Eating in Nerja, telephone code: 95, postal code: 29780.

The entire Costa del Tourismo is crowded during peak season. While August is most difficult, July 15 through September 15 is tight, since this is when Spanish workers head for the beaches. In high season, arrive early, let the tourist office help you, or follow a local woman home (a *casa particular*). Any other time of year, you'll find Nerja has plenty of comfy low-rise, easygoing, resort-type hotels and rooms. Nerja room prices vary with the season.

Habitaciónes de José Luis Jaime Escobar Compresores y Voladuras (cheap, Mendez Nuñez 12, tel. 252 29 30) is clean, friendly, and really local . . . worth the communication struggles. It's in the residential section about a 5-minute walk inland, near the corner of C. America and Mendez Nuñez. The kids of the family always seem to be dressed up and heading off to some festival, dance, or concert. If no one answers, ask at the nearby bar.

Within three blocks of the Balcony of Europe, more normal, boxy, professional, and hotelesque are **Hostal Residencia Don Peque** (inexpensive, Diputación 13, tel. 252 13 18, air-conditioned, run by Sr. Bautista, who speaks some English and reminds me so much of my Uncle Ron), the **Hostal Atembeni** (cheap-inexpensive, Diputación 12, tel. 252 13 41), the **Hostal Residencia Mena** (cheap-inexpensive, some sea-view rooms with balconies, El Barrio 15, tel. 252 05 41), and, most central and hotelesque of all, the **Hotel CalaBella** (inexpensive, Puerta del Mar 8, tel. 252 07 00, fax 252 0700) with some sea-view rooms.

Your cheapest and often most interesting bet is private accommodations (*casas particulares*). Prowl the residential streets within about six blocks around C. La Parra. Ask around.

Your most memorable splurge is the **Balcón de Europa** (expensive, with the prestigious address, Balcón de Europa 1, tel. 252 08 00, fax 252 4490) right on the water and on the square. The local parador is even pricier (12,000 ptas, tel. 252 00 50, fax 252 1997).

You'll find plenty of lively eateries around the central Balcony of Europe. Of course, the farther inland you go, the more local and cheaper it gets, with sea views thumbtacked onto the wall. Next to the Hotel CalaBella is a good cafeteria restaurant with great views. The **Cou-Cou Rôtisserie** is a good place if you feel like half a chicken.

Sightseeing Highlight, near Nerja

▲▲The Caves of Nerja—These caves have the most impressive pile of stalactites and stalagmites I've seen anywhere in Europe, with huge cathedrals and domed stadiums of caverns filled with expertly backlit formations and very cavey music—well worth the time and money (daily 10:30-18:00, tel. 952 0076, shorter hours in off-season, 400 ptas).

Granada

See Day 20.

DAY 20

GRANADA

You will have all day to explore this city's incomparable Alhambra palace, to let your senses off their leash in the exotic Arabic Quarter, to flirt with the Gypsies, and to stroll with the Granadines.

Suggested Schedule	
8:00	Breakfast.
9:00	Wander, stroll, and shop in pedestrian zone.
11:00	Tour royal chapel and cathedral.
12:30	Picnic in Generalife, enjoy garden.
14:00	Tour Alhambra.

Note: To save a day or gain time for Toledo, do the Alhambra pronto and drive 6 hours to Toledo. Train travelers should take the night train to Madrid for the morning connection to Toledo.

Orientation

It has been said, "There's nothing crueler than being blind in Granada" (unless it's being alive in Cleveland). Granada is a fascinating city, with a beautiful, often snow-capped, Sierra Nevada backdrop, the Alhambra fortress glowing red in the evening, and Spain's best-preserved Moorish Quarter. This is our Moorish pilgrimage. But the town tourist brochure may have overdone it just a bit when it reports, "It can be said that Granada, rather than being a product of the culture of the Moorish civilization in Spain, was the shaper and builder of that culture and of the spiritual and human structure of the very people themselves. And all of this thanks to its mysterious and magical power of suggestion. When the nomadic and warlike Moors burst into the Iberian Peninsula, they were a hard, austere, fighting race, driven by religious fanaticism. But when Ferdinand and Isabella reconquered the city they found a sensual, refined, dreaming race, whose chief delights were in art and nature."

Granada

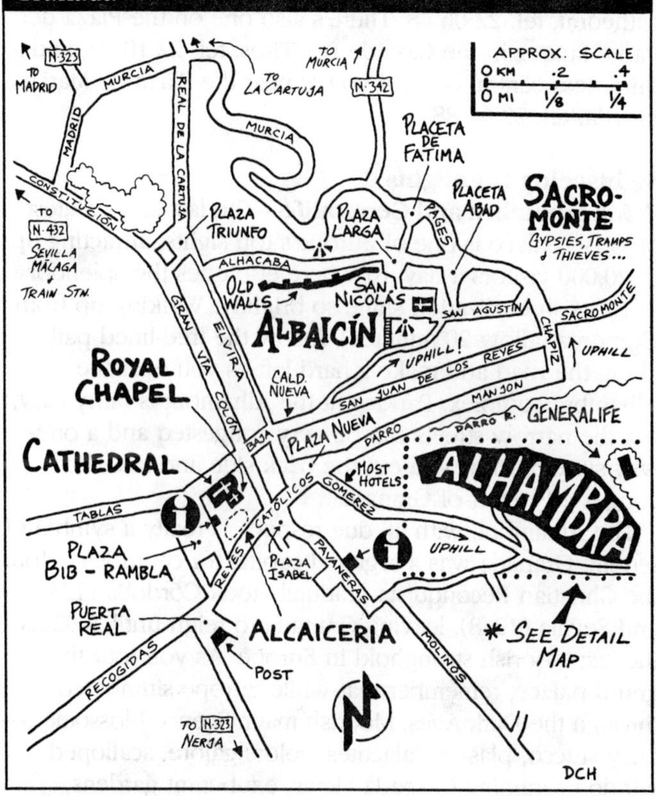

Granada is a sizable city of over 200,000 people. But for a quick visit, it's all within a 20-minute walk of Plaza Nueva, where dogs wave their tails to the rhythm of the street musicians. This center of the historic city is in the Darro River valley which separates two hills, one with the great Moorish palace, the Alhambra, and the other with the best old Arabic or Moorish Quarter in Spain, the Albaicín. To the southeast are the cathedral, royal chapel, and Alcaicería (Arab market) where the city's two main drags (Gran Vía de Colón and Reyes Católicos) come together. By the way, "Granada" means pomegranate and you'll see the city's symbol everywhere.

There are three Turismos to choose from here, all with erratic hours and long lunches: the most central of them is on Libreros 2, just off Plaza de Bib-Rambla next to the cathedral, tel. 22 06 88. There's also one on the Plaza del Padre Suarez in the Casa de Los Tiros, tel. 22 10 22, and a third, less-central office if you're near the Plaza de Mariana Pineda, tel. 22 66 88.

Sightseeing Highlights

▲▲▲Alhambra and Generalife—The last and greatest Moorish palace is one of Europe's top sights, attracting up to 20,000 visitors a day. Nowhere else does the splendor of Moorish civilization shine so brightly. Walking up from Gomerez (allow 20 minutes), follow the tree-lined path along the road and make a hard left as you near the Alhambra complex. Parking at the Alhambra is fairly easy, but the narrow streets can be very congested and a one-way system sends you out the back side and into the congested center of Granada.

The Alhambra, with all due respect, is really a symbol of retreat. Granada was a regional capital for centuries before the Christian Reconquista gradually took Córdoba (1236) and Sevilla (1248), leaving Granada to reign until 1492 as the last Moorish stronghold in Europe. As you tour this grand palace, remember that while Europe slumbered through the Dark Ages, Moorish magnificence blossomed—busy stucco, plaster stalactites, colors galore, scalloped windows framing Granada views, exuberant gardens, and water, water everywhere. Water, so rare and precious in most of the Islamic world, was the purest symbol of life to the Moors. The Alhambra is decorated with water standing still, running slow and fast, cascading, and drip-dropping playfully.

Your tour of the Alhambra has four sections: Charles V's Palace, the Alcazaba or old fort, the Palacios Nazaries (Moorish Palace), and the Generalife garden. You basically follow the arrows. Try to avoid arriving as it opens—when countless tour groups do. The afternoons and evenings are less crowded. Buy the helpful guidebook (500 ptas, great layout plan included) at the small shop outside and below the ticket room. Take your time to read it and understand the layout and history of this

Alhambra

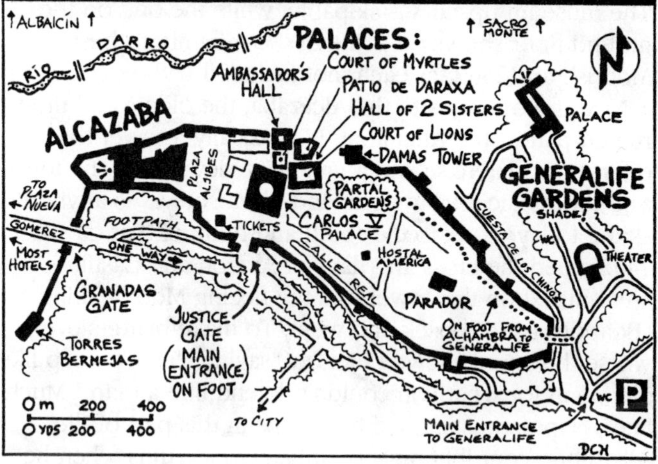

remarkable sight before entering. Once in the Palacios Nazaries you'll find it difficult at times to get oriented. There's a clean WC downstairs from the ticket room. All parts of the Alhambra are open daily 9:00 to 20:00, until 18:00 on Sunday and off-season, and on summer Tuesday, Thursday, and Saturday nights from 22:00 to 24:00, 600 ptas. Your ticket is good only for the date stamped on it.

The new computerized ticketing system regulates the number of people in the Alhambra's highlight, the Palacios Nazaries, by issuing you a half-hour window of time during which you must enter. You can tour the other sights with the same ticket at your leisure. The key to a successful Palacios Nazaries visit is avoiding large tour groups. Hang out by the entrance 10 minutes before your half-hour to be the first one in for your platooned time. By hustling ahead, you'll enjoy the rooms in relative peace.

Start your tour with Charles V's Palace, impressive but sadly out of place. Remind yourself that it's only natural for a conquering king to build his own palace over his victim's palace. This is the most impressive Renaissance building you'll see in Spain, designed by Pedro Machuca, a student of Michelangelo's. Sit in the circular courtyard and imagine being here for one of Charles's bullfights. The museum upstairs is skipable, while the one on the ground floor shows off some of the Alhambra's best Moorish art (250 ptas each, not included with your ticket)

Next, follow signs to the Alcazaba, the oldest and most-ruined part of the Alhambra. It's basically a tower that offers some exercise and a great city view. From the top find the Albaicín view point and Plaza Nueva. Is anybody skiing today? Look to the south and think of that day in 1492 when the cross and flags of Aragon and Castile were raised on this tower and the fleeing Moorish king (Boabdil) looked back and wept. To make matters even worse, his mom chewed him out, saying, "Don't weep like a woman for what you couldn't defend like a man." Much later, Napoleon stationed his troops in this part of the Alhambra, contributing substantially to its ruins when he left. Follow the arrows down and around to the Palacios Nazaries, the middle finger still remaining on your ticket.

Be mindful of your window of time and step into the jewel of the Alhambra, the Moorish royal palace, Palacios Nazaries. This is our best possible look at the refined and elegant civilization of Al-Andalus. If you can imagine a few tapestries, carpets, and some ivory-studded wooden furniture, the place is much as it was for the Moorish kings. Remember the palace themes: water, no images, and ornate "stalactite" ceilings throughout—and no signs telling you where you are.

From the Court of Myrtles (with the long goldfish pond), study the ceiling of the Hall of the Boat (and guess how it got its name). Beyond that, don't miss the beautifully decorated Hall of the Ambassadors with its Albaicín views. Then find your way into the much-photographed Court of the Lions. Six hundred years ago, the Moors could read the Koranic poetry that ornaments this court and could understand the symbolism of the enclosed garden (the realization of paradise or truth) and the twelve lions (signs of the zodiac, months, and so on). Imagine, they enjoyed this part of the palace even more than we do today.

Untie yourself, and the river of tourists will float you into the gardens. On the hillside to the east, with carefully pruned hedges, is the Generalife and, if you drove, your car. Upon leaving the Palacios Nazaries, walk straight through the gardens; this eventually leads around to the Generalife.

Don't miss the summer palace, the Generalife (pronounced: henneraw-LEEF-ay). This most perfect Arabian garden in Andalusia was the summer home of the Moorish kings, the closest thing on earth to the Koran's description of heaven. Consider a picnic in the Generalife.

▲▲Albaicín—This is the best old Moorish quarter in Spain, with thousands of colorful corners, flowery patios, and shady lanes to soothe the twentieth-century-mangled visitor. Climb high to the San Nicolás church for the best view of the Alhambra, especially early in the morning or at sunset. Go on a photo safari. Ignore the Gypsies. Women shouldn't wander alone after dark.

The easiest approach is to taxi to Plaza Larga and explore from there. For the quickest, most scenic walk up the hill, leave from the west end of the Plaza Nueva on Calle Elvira, then turn right on tiny Calderería Nueva. Follow the stepped street as it slants, winds, and zigzags up the hill, veering left at every uncertain turn. Near the crest, turn right on Camino Nuevo de San Nicolás, walking several blocks to the steps leading up to the church's view point (a must). From there, walk north (away from the Alhambra), to the small street that leads from the upper left corner of the small square past the Biblioteca Municipal, then drop down to the right through the old Moorish wall into Plaza Larga, the tiny city square. Stop here for something to eat or drink. This is the heart of the Albaicín. Try to poke into one of the old churches. They are very plain, in order to go easy on the Muslim converts who weren't used to being surrounded by images as they worshiped. From here, you can walk to Sacromonte.

Sacromonte—Europe's most disgusting tourist trap, famous for its cave-dwelling, foot-stomping, flamenco-dancing Gypsies, is a snakepit of con artists. You'll be teased, taken, and turned away. Venture in only for the curiosity and leave your money in the hotel. Enjoy flamenco in Sevilla. Gypsies have gained a reputation (all over Europe) for targeting tourists. Be careful. Even mothers with big eyes and a baby on each arm manage to find a spare hand to sneak into your pocket.

▲Royal Chapel (Capilla Real) and Cathedral—Without a doubt Granada's top Christian sight, this lavish chapel holds the dreams—and bodies—of Queen Isabella and King Ferdinand. Besides the royal tombs (walk down the steps), you'll find some great Flemish art (Memling), paintings by Botticelli and Perugino, the royal jewels, Ferdinand's sword, and the most lavish interior money could buy 500 years ago. Because of its speedy completion, the chapel is an unusually harmonious piece of architecture (open daily 10:30-13:00, 16:00-19:00, 150 ptas).

The cathedral, the only Renaissance church in Spain, is a welcome break from the twisted Gothic and tortured baroque of so many Spanish churches. Spacious, symmetrical, and lit by a stained-glass-filled rotunda, it's well worth a visit. The Renaissance facade and paintings of the Virgin in the rotunda are by Granada's own Alonso Cano (1601-1661) (open daily 10:30-13:00, 16:00-19:00, 150 ptas). The coin-op lighting is worthwhile. Fiercely ignore the obnoxious ladies with roses who want to read your palms and empty your pockets. The mesh of tiny shopping lanes between these buildings and the Calle Reyes Católicos is the Alcaicería, the site of the old Moorish market.

Lotería de Ciegos—In Granada you may notice blind men selling lottery tickets with nerve-racking shouts. This is a form of welfare. The locals never expect to win, it's just sort of a social responsibility to help these people out. The saying goes, "Dale limosna, mujer, porque no hay nada que ser ciego en Granada" (Give him a coin, woman, because there's nothing worse than being blind in Granada).

Carthusian Monastery (La Cartuja)—Another church with an interior that looks like it came out of a can of Cool Whip, La Cartuja is nicknamed the "Christian Alhambra" for its elaborate white baroque stucco work. Notice the gruesome paintings of martyrs placidly meeting their grisly fates (in the rooms just off the cloister). It's located a mile out of town, on the way to Madrid—go north on Gran Vía and follow the signs or take bus #8 (open 10:00-19:00, Sunday 10:00-12:00).

International Festival of Music and Dance—From mid-June to mid-July, you can enjoy some of the world's best classical music in classic settings in the Alhambra at reasonable prices.

Sleeping in Granada, telephone code: 958, see postal codes below.

In Granada, I try to sleep in places on the Plaza Nueva or on Cuesta de Gomerez, the road leading off the square up to the Alhambra. In July and August, rooms and sunstroke victims are plentiful. September, October, and November are more crowded, and you'll want to arrive early or call ahead. Upon arrival, drive, bus, or taxi to the Plaza Nueva. You'll find many small, reasonable hotels to choose from within a few blocks up Cuesta de Gomerez. Here are my choices; all except the last four are on or near the square. Postal code for the first five hotels is 18009.

Hostal Residencia Britz (inexpensive, Plaza Nueva y Gomerez 1, tel. 22 36 52) is a no-nonsense place, ideally located right on the square with an elevator and some fine view rooms.

Hostal Landazuri (cheap, Cuesta de Gomerez 24, tel. 22 14 06), run by friendly, English-speaking Matilda Landazuri and her two children, is plain and clean. It's a bit faded and yellow but has a great roof garden with an Alhambra view and a helpful management. The Landazuris also run a good cheap restaurant and bar.

Hostal Navarro Ramos (cheap, Cuesta de Gomerez 21, tel. 25 05 55) is cleaner and better-assembled than Landazuri but with less warmth and character.

The tiny **Hostal Viena** (cheap, Hospital de S. Ana 2, just off Cuesta de Gomerez, tel. 22 18 59), with three doubles and one shower, is run by an English-speaking family.

Hostal Residencia Gomerez (very cheap, showers down the hall, Cuesta Gomerez 10, one floor up, tel. 22 44 37) is run by English-speaking Sigfrido Sanchez de

León de Torres (who will explain to you how Spanish surnames work if you've got the time). Clean and basic, and listed in nearly every country's student travel guidebook, this is your best cheapie.

Right on the colorful Plaza Nueva is **Hotel Residencia Macia** (moderate, Plaza Nueva 4, 18010 Granada, tel. 22 75 36, fax 28 55 91). This classy, hotelesque place is clean and modern and has a distant garage, and English is spoken. It comes with TVs and phones in the room, a Yankee breakfast buffet, and your choice of a view on the square or a quiet room.

I don't know why people want to stay up near the Alhambra, but here are three popular options. The stately old **Hotel Washington Irving** (expensive, Paseo del Generalife 2, tel. 22 75 50, fax 22 88 40) is pleasant and spacious, offering the best reasonable beds in this prestigious neighborhood. There are two famous, overpriced, and difficult-to-get-a-room-in hotels actually within the Alhambra grounds. The **Parador Nacional San Francisco** (22,000 ptas, tel. 22 14 40, fax 22 22 64) is a converted fifteenth-century convent, usually called Spain's premier parador. You must book ahead to spend the night in this lavishly located, stodgy, classy, and historic place. Do drop in for coffee or a drink. Next to the parador is **Hostal America** (expensive, tel. 227471), which is small (just 14 rooms), elegant, snooty, and very popular. Advance bookings are necessary, and you are virtually required to have dinner there.

Back in the real world, on a lively but traffic-free square behind the cathedral, a five-minute walk from Plaza Nueva, is **Hotel Los Tilos** (inexpensive, Plaza Bib-Rambla 4, tel. 26 67 12, fax 26 68 01). The place feels and smells a bit like an old elementary school, but some rooms have balconies over the square and it's in a great shopping and people-watching area.

Eating in Granada

The most interesting reasonable meals are a steep walk up in the Albaicín quarter. From the San Nicolas view point, head a few blocks north (away from the Alhambra) to

Café-Bar Higuera, just off Placeta Fatima. For a memorable orgy of seafood specialties at a reasonable price, at great outdoor tables in a colorful square atmosphere, eat at **El Ladrillo** (Placeta de Fatima just off Calle Pages in the Albaicín). Their *media barca* (half boat) is a fishy feast that can stuff two to the gills.

For tapas, prowl through the bars around the Plaza del Campo del Príncipe. For a cheap and decent menu on Cuesta de Gomerez, try **Restaurante Landazuri** (at #24) or the restaurant next to the Residencial Gomerez.

There are plenty of good places around the Plaza Nueva. Try **Mesón Andaluz** at Elvira 10 (new, clean, air-conditioned, with few tourists) or **Restaurante Bar León** just north of Plaza Nueva at Calle Pan 3 for good tapas, cheap meals, and a friendly atmosphere.

DAY 21

THROUGH LA MANCHA TO TOLEDO

Today's goal is to travel 250 miles north, lunching in La Mancha country and arriving early enough to get comfortably set up and oriented in the historic, artistic, and spiritual capital of Spain—Toledo.

Suggested Schedule—By Car

8:00	Breakfast and drive north.
12:00	Picnic lunch at Consuegra, tour castle and windmills.
14:00	Drive on to Toledo.
16:00	Arrive in Toledo, confirm plans at tourist office, set up, tour cathedral, enjoy the paseo, and, if you feel like pig, have a roast suckling one in a restaurant in Toledo's dark medieval quarter.

The Route: Granada to Toledo (250 miles, 5 hours)
The drive north from Granada is long, hot, and boring. Start early to minimize the heat, and make the best time you can in the direction of Madrid. Follow signs for Madrid/Jaen/N323 into what some call the Spanish Nebraska—La Mancha. After Puerto Lapice, you'll see the Toledo exit.

By Bus and Train
Bus and rail service to points north of Granda is dismal. The best public transport option to follow my route is the overnight Granada-Madrid train (about 23:15-8:00). From Madrid's Atocha station there are 15 Cercanias trains a day to Toledo, (allow 60 to 80 minutes). You can take the night train more directly to Toledo, changing in Aranjuez. If you saw Toledo earlier on your trip, consider the night train to Barcelona via Cordoba (leave Granada 1705, arrive 1105). Make your arrangements in Granada at the Granada RENFE office on Calle Reyes Católicos 63, one block down from Plaza Nueva (open 9:00-13:30 and 17:00-19:00, tel. 22 34 97). Toledo's train station, a long hike from town,

is easily connected to the center by buses #5 and #6. The bus station, just below Plaza de Zocodover, is closer to town and served by the same buses.

La Mancha

Nowhere else is Spain so vast, flat, and radically monotonous. La Mancha, Arabic for "parched earth," makes you feel small . . . lost in rough seas of olive green polka dots. Random buildings look like houses and hotels that were thrown off some heavenly Monopoly board. It's a land where road-kill is left to rot, where hitchhikers wear red dresses and aim to take *you* for the ride. It's a rough world, where ham and cheese sandwiches are the local specialty, and bugs seem to ricochet off the windshield and keep on flying.

This is the setting of Cervantes's *Don Quixote*, published in the seventeenth century, after England sank the Armada and the Spanish empire began its decline. Cervantes's star character fought doggedly for good, for justice, and against the fall of Spain. Ignoring reality, Don Quixote was a hero fighting a hopeless battle. Stark La Mancha is the perfect stage for this sad and futile fight.

The epitome of Don Quixote country, the town of Consuegra must be the La Mancha Cervantes had in mind. Drive up to the ruined twelfth-century castle and joust with a windmill. It's hot and buggy here, but the powerful view overlooking the village, with its sun-bleached light red roofs, modern concrete reality, and harsh, windy silence, makes for a profound picnic before driving on to Toledo (1 hour). The castle belonged to the Knights of St. John (twelfth and thirteenth centuries) and is associated with their trip to Jerusalem during the Crusades. Originally built from the ruins of a nearby Roman Circus, it has been newly restored. Sorry, the windmills are post-Cervantes, only 200 to 300 years old.

If you've seen windmills, the next castle north (above Almonacid), 12 km from Toledo, is more interesting than the Consuegra castle (and free). Follow the ruined lane past the ruined church up to the ruined castle. The jovial locals hike up with kids and kites. Welcome back to Castile.

A desert swim? Fifteen minutes north of Granada you'll see a popular swimming spot just off the highway. Farther north, 30 miles east of Manzanares, are the fourteen deep blue lagoons of Ruidera at the beautiful headwaters of the Río Guadino.

Toledo

See Day 22.

DAY 22

TOLEDO AND "HOME" TO MADRID

Tour Toledo, a place of such beauty and historic importance that the entire city was declared a national monument. Finally, you'll complete your 22-day circle through Spain and Portugal by returning to Madrid.

Suggested Schedule—By Car	
8:30	Breakfast, check out of hotel.
9:30	Market, Santa Cruz and shopping or more sightseeing (Santo Tomé, El Greco's house, Alcázar, all open until 14:00).
14:00	Lunch, siesta.
17:00	Return to Madrid, where you have a hotel reserved and paid for at the beginning of your trip or where you'll catch the night train to Barcelona. (Or spend another evening and night in Toledo, Spain's most magically medieval big town.)

The Route: Toledo to Madrid (40 miles)

It's a speedy *autovía* north, past one last bull billboard, to Madrid. The highways converge into M30, which circles Madrid. Follow it to the left ("Nor y Oeste") and take the "Plaza de España" exit to get back to the Gran Vía. If you're airport-bound, keep heading into Madrid until you see the airplane symbol (N-II). I drove from Toledo's Alcazar to Madrid's airport in just under an hour (but then, I'm a travel writer). Arriving by car, view the city from many angles along the Circunvalación road across the Tajo Gorge. Drive to the Parador Conde de Orgaz just south of town for about the same view as El Greco's famous *Portrait of Toledo* (from the balcony).

Enter the city by the north gate and park in the open-air guarded lot (cheap, but not safe overnight) or in one of three garages. The garage just past the Alcázar is easy and as central as you need (1,000 ptas/24 hours), or park free in the lot just down the street from the garage.

Toledo

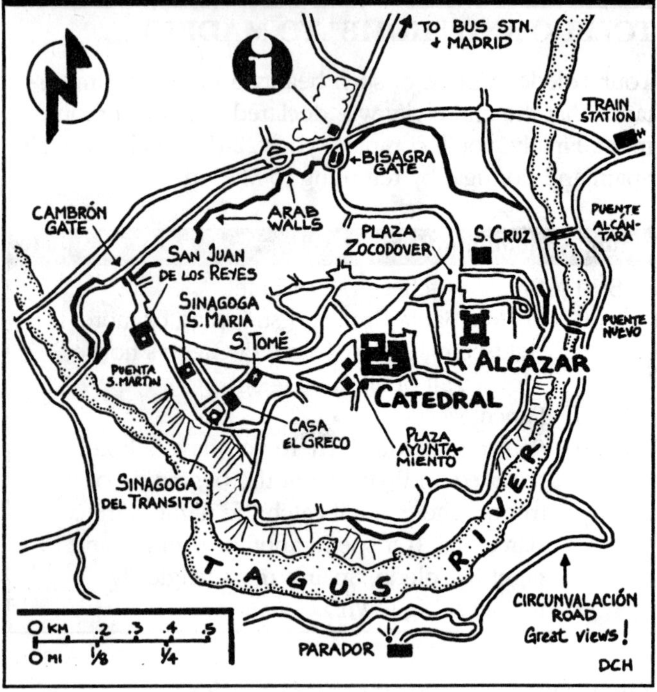

By Bus and Train

Buses and trains leave almost hourly for Madrid, from which the rest of Europe is accessible. Seven trains per day connect Madrid and Barcelona in about 8.5 hours. Train information: 925/22 30 99 or 22 12 72, bus information: 22 29 61.

Toledo

Spain's historic capital is 2,000 years of tangled history—Roman, Visigothic, Moorish, and Christian—crowded onto a high, rocky perch bordered on three sides by the Tajo River. It's so well preserved that the Spanish government has forbidden any modern exteriors. The rich mix of Jewish, Moorish, and Christian heritage makes it one of Europe's art capitals.

Toledo was a Visigothic capital way back in 554 and Spain's political capital until 1561, when it reached its natural limits of growth, as defined by the Tajo River Gorge. The king moved to more spacious Madrid. Today, in spite of tremendous tourist crowds, Toledo just takes care of its history and remains much as it was when El Greco called it home, and painted it, 400 years ago. If you like El Greco, you'll love Toledo.

Toledo Orientation

Lassoed into a tight tangle of streets by the sharp bend of the Tajo River (called the Tagus where it hits the Atlantic, in Lisbon), Toledo has the most medievally confusing street plan in Spain. But it's a small town, with only 50,000 people, and a joy to be lost in. Because of the town's popularity with tourists, major sights are well sign-posted, and most locals will politely point you in the right direction.

Orient yourself with a walk past Toledo's main sights. Starting in the very central Plaza de Zocodover, walk southwest along the Calle de Comércio. After passing the cathedral on your left, follow the signs to Santo Tomé and the cluster of other sights. This walk shows you that the visitors' city is basically along one small but central street. Still, I routinely get completely turned around. Knowing that the town is bounded by the river on three sides and is very small, I wander, happily lost. When it's time to get somewhere, I pull out the map.

The tourist office just outside the north wall gate, which has a much handier branch on the Plaza de Zocodover, has maps and accommodations lists (open Monday-Saturday 10:00-18:00, Sunday 10:00-15:00, tel. 925/22 08 43). The readable local guide, *Toledo, Its Art and Its History,* sold all over town at 550 ptas for the small version, explains all the sights (which generally provide no explanation) and gives you a photo to point at and say, "¿Dónde está?" when you tire of being lost.

Sightseeing Highlights—Toledo

▲▲El Greco—Born on Crete and trained in Venice, Domenikos Theotocopoulos (tongue-tied friends just called him "The Greek") came to Spain to get a job decorating El Escorial. He failed there but succeeded in Toledo where he spent the last 37 years of his life. He mixed all three regional influences into his palette. From his Greek homeland, he absorbed the solemn, abstract style of icons. In Venice, he learned the bold use of color and dramatic style of the later Renaissance. These styles were then fused in the fires of fanatic Spanish Catholic devotion.

Not bound by the realism so important to his contemporaries, El Greco painted dramatic visions of striking colors and figures, with bodies unnatural and elongated as though stretched between heaven and earth. He painted souls, not faces. His work is almost as fresh to us as the art of today, thoroughly "modern" in its disregard of realism.

▲▲▲**Cathedral**—Holy Toledo! Spain's leading Catholic city has a magnificent cathedral. While the exterior is crowded into this crowded city and hard to appreciate, the interior is so lofty, rich, and vast that it grabs you by the vocal chords and all you can do is whisper, "Wow." Walk through this holy redwood forest. Find any old pillar to sit under and imagine when the light bulbs were candles and the tourists were pilgrims . . . before the "no photo" signs, when every window provided spiritual as well as physical light. The cathedral is basically Gothic but took over 200 years to build (1226-1493). So you'll see a mix of styles, Gothic, Renaissance, and baroque . . . elaborate wrought-iron work, lavish wood carving, window after colorful window of 500-year-old stained glass, and a sacristy with a collection of paintings that would put any museum on the map.

Don't miss the unique Transparente. In the 1700s, a hole was cut into the ceiling to let a sunbeam brighten the mass. Melding this big hole into the Gothic church presented a challenge that resulted in a baroque masterpiece. Study this riot of angels doing flip-flops, babies breathing thin air, bottoms of feet, and gilded sunbursts. It makes you hope no one falls down. I like it, as, I guess, did the long-dead cardinal whose hat hangs from the edge of the hole (choosing the place in which their hat will hang till it rots is a perk only cardinals enjoy).

If you're there between 9:30 and 9:45 you can peek into the otherwise-locked-up Mozarabic Chapel (Capilla Mozarabe) to witness the Visigothic mass, the oldest surviving Christian ritual in Western Europe. You're welcome to partake in this impressive example of peaceful coexistence of faiths, but once the door closes you're in for 30 minutes of Latin.

While the basic cathedral is free, seeing the great art requires a ticket. The cathedral's sacristy has over twenty El Grecos, masterpieces by Goya, Titian, Rubens, Velázquez, and Bellini, and a carved St. Francis that could change your life. The choir (*coro*) is elaborately carved inside and out. Notice the scenes from the conquest of Granada. The treasury's biggie is the 10-foot-high, 430-pound monstrance (by Arfe), which is carried through Toledo in the Corpus Christi parade. It's made of gold and silver, much of which came in on Columbus's first load home. The chapter house (*Sala Capitular*) has a rich gilt ceiling, interesting Bible story-telling frescoes, and a pictorial review of 1,900 years of Toledo archbishops.

This confusing collage of great Spanish art deserves a guided tour. Hire a private guide (or freeload), or at least follow a local guidebook. On my tour I felt my guide's national pride saying, "Look at this great stuff! Why do you tourists get so excited about Michelangelo and Leonardo? Take a look at Spain!" It is interesting how little attention we give the art of Spain's Golden Age (the cathedral is open daily 10:30-13:00 and 15:30-19:00, 300 ptas).

Fernando Garrido, a guide and interpreter who runs a fine jewelry shop in the cathedral cloister (at the entrance, where you buy your cathedral tickets), gives an excellent 1-hour tour for 4,500 ptas. He is an entertaining and friendly character (a kind of Rodrigo Dangerfield) and has a wealth of information (tel. 22 40 07). Say "Buenos días" to him, check out his shop, and consider enlisting his help. If you can't take his tour, maybe he'll loan you a guidebook to the cathedral he loves.

▲▲▲Santa Cruz Museum—This great Renaissance hospital building holds 22 El Grecos and much more in a tasteful, stately, old, classical, music-filled setting (open

Monday-Saturday 10:00-18:30, Sunday 10:00-14:00, 200 ptas, free English pamphlet. No photos allowed, but individual slides are available).

▲**Alcázar**—A huge, entirely rebuilt, former imperial residence dominating the Toledo skyline, it became a kind of right-wing Alamo of Spain's Civil War when a force of Franco's Nationalists (and hundreds of hostages) were besieged for two months. Finally, after many fierce but futile Republican attacks, Franco sent in an army that took Toledo and freed the Alcázar. The place was rebuilt and glorified under Franco. Today you can see its Civil War exhibits, giving you an interesting, and right-wing, look at the horrors of Spain's recent past (open 9:30-13:30 and 16:00-19:30, closed Sunday and Monday afternoon, 125 ptas).

▲**Santo Tomé**—A simple chapel with, probably, El Greco's most exciting painting. The powerful *Burial of the Count of Orgaz* merges heaven and earth in a way only "The Greek" could. It's so good to see a painting left where the artist put it 400 years ago. Sit here for a while—let it perform. Each face is a detailed portrait. Notice the artist's self-portrait looking straight at you (sixth figure in from the left). The boy in the foreground is El Greco's son. (Open 10:00-13:45 and 15:30-17:45, 100 ptas.)

▲**El Greco's House**—It wasn't really El Greco's, but it is really a house, giving you an interesting look at the interior of a traditionally furnished Renaissance-period home. You'll see El Greco's masterful *View of Toledo* and portraits of the apostles. (Open 10:00-14:00 and 16:00-18:00, closed Sunday afternoon and Monday, 200 ptas.)

Sinagoga del Transito—This part of Toledo's Jewish past, built in 1366, is located next to El Greco's house on Calle de los Reyes Católicos (same hours as the house).

Other sights are listed and explained on the tourist information map. Most of these are closed on Monday.

Shopping—Toledo probably sells as many souvenirs as any city in Spain. This is the best place to buy old-looking swords, armor, maces, medieval-looking three-legged stools, and other nouveau antiques. It's also Spain's damascene center, where, for centuries, craftsmen have inlaid black steelware with gold, silver, and copper wire. At Calle Ciudad 19, near the cathedral and Plaza Ayuntamiento, you can see swords and knives being made in the workshop of English-speaking Mariano Zamorano. Judging by what's left of his hand, his knives are very good.

El Martes is Toledo's outdoor market, on Tuesdays, as the name suggests, from 9:00 to 13:00.

Sleeping in Toledo, telephone code: 925, postal code: 45001.

Madrid day-trippers clog the sunlit cobbles, but Toledo's medieval moon rises after dark. Even though Toledo accommodations can be a problem, spend the night. Cheap places are dreary and scattered. Well-located, moderately priced places are not a good value. To stay in the old center, you'll have to splurge or make do with a musty or rundown place. Classier places adjust rates according to the season: July 15 through September 15 is high, November through February is low. There are no rooms for rent in private homes.

Hotel Maravilla (inexpensive-moderate, Plaza de Barrio Rey 7, just behind the Plaza de Zocodover, tel. 22 33 00; Irene speaks English) is wonderfully central, quiet, convenient, and even with its dark narrow halls and borderline rundown rooms, it offers the best middle-range value in the old center.

Hotel Carlos V (inexpensive-moderate, Pl. Horno Magdalena 3, tel. 22 21 00, fax 22 21 05) is ideally located overlooking the cathedral, between the Alcázar and the Zocodover. It suffers from the obligatory stuffiness of a correct hotel but has bright, pleasant rooms and elegant bathrooms. Nearby, across from the Alcázar, is **Hotel Alfonso VI** (expensive, General Moscardo 2, tel. 22 26 00, fax 21 44 58), a big, touristy, English-speaking place with large, airy rooms, tour groups, and souvenirs for sale all over the lobby. I hate to steer anyone there, but in central Toledo you take what you can.

Fonda Segovia (cheap, Calle de Recoletos 2; on a tiny square from Zocodover go down Calle de la Sillería and take the second right; tel. 21 11 24) is cheap, quiet, clean, and very central. It's also old, rickety, and dingy, with saggy beds and memorable balconies. Duck your head; the ancient ceilings are low. Teresa's smile shrinks the language barrier.

Two quiet, central, and simple places just next to Hotel Carlos V are **Hostal Residencia Labrador** (inexpensive, Juan Labrador 16, tel. 22 26 20) and the smaller, cheerier, family-run **Pensión Lumbreras** (cheap, Calle Juan Labrador 9, tel. 22 15 71).

Hostal Descalzos (inexpensive, Calle de los Descalzos 30, tel. 22 28 88) is bright, new, comfortable, in all the budget guides, and the best middle-range room in the old town. Unfortunately, it's way down by the river, near what they call El Greco's house.

The best splurge in town is the **Hostal de Cardenal** (expensive, Paseo de Recardo 24, near Puerta Bisagra, tel. 22 24 90, fax 22 29 91). This seventeenth-century cardinal's palace built into the Toledo wall is quiet and elegant, with a cool garden and a fine restaurant. The only drawback of this poor man's parador is its location, at the noisy, dusty old gate of Toledo.

For those who want it all and will leave the town center and pay anything to get it, Toledo's **Parador** is one of Spain's most famous, enjoying the same Toledo view El Greco made famous from across the Tajo canyon (11,000-15,000 ptas, depending on view, no address necessary, tel. 22 18 50, fax 22 51 66).

Hostales los Gavilánes (moderate, Calle Marqués de Mendigorría 14, next to the Plaza de Toros, tel. 21 16 28 or 22 46 22) is bright and modern, with 15 very comfortable rooms and easy parking outside town on the main drag to Madrid, a 10-minute walk from the old gate. Check out their sweet suite. Cheaper but nowhere near as good or friendly is the neighboring **Hostal Madrid** (inexpensive, Calle Marqués de Mendigorría 7, tel. 22 11 14). The youth hostel, **Residencia Juvenil San Servando** (San Servando castle near the train station, over the Puente Viejo outside town; tel. 22 45 54), is lavish but cheap, with small rooms, swimming pool, views, and a good management. They can direct you to nearby budget beds when the hostel is full.

Eating in Toledo

Eating cheaply in Toledo is tough, but the romance of this town always puts me in the mood for a good splurge—specifically, suckling pigs . . . roasted. Try **Casa Aurelio** (2,000 pta menu, Plaza Ayuntamiento 8, near the cathedral; call 22 77 16 for a reservation) for great food, moderate prices, and classy atmosphere. Another fine splurge is a meal in the palatial **Hostal de Cardenal Restaurante** (see Sleeping in Toledo). This restaurant serves wonderfully prepared local specialties. **Restaurante-Meson Palacios** on Alfonso IV is another good bet.

You'll find several budget restaurants behind the Zocodover. **Bar Parrilla** is an easy place to put away a few tapas (bar on ground floor, decent restaurant upstairs on Plaza de Barrio Rey; take the alley from Zocodover past Café Casa Telesfor to a small square). If Angel's working, give him a high five and ask for a free shrimp.

For breakfast, **Cafetería Croissanterie Repostería** (between the Zocodover and the cathedral at Comércio 38) serves fresh croissants and churros. These churros are as good as any—and they still rival lutefisk as the leading European national dish of penitence. For heartier appetites, they serve a huge tortilla MacMuffin. And I can't walk past the place without picking up one of their Napolitana de Chocolates.

For a sweet and romantic evening moment, get one of these chocolate donuts (or whatever suits your sweet tooth) and head down to the cathedral. Sit on the Plaza del Ayuntamiento (there's a comfortable perch ten yards down the lane from the huge granite bowling ball) with the fountain on your right, Spain's best-looking city hall behind you, and her top cathedral, built back when Toledo was Spain's capital, shining brightly against the black night sky before you.

For Toledo's famous almond-fruity sweet marzipan, try **Casa Telesforo** at Plaza de Zocodover 17, open until

22:00. The bars and cafés on Plaza de Zocodover are reasonable. Sit outside and enjoy the people-watching.

Picnics are best assembled at the Mercado Municipal on Plaza Mayor (on the Alcázar side of the cathedral). This is a fun market to prowl, even if you don't need food. If you need some more giant communion wafers (see Salamanca), one of the stalls sells crispy bags of Obleas.

That's my idea of the most travel thrills Spain and Portugal can give you in 2 to 22 days. I hope you have a great trip—and many more.

POSTTOUR OPTIONS

BARCELONA

Barcelona is (at least) Spain's second city and the capital of the proud and distinct region of Catalunya (Catalonia). With Franco's fascism now history, Catalunya flags wave proud again. The local language and culture are on a roll in Spain's most cosmopolitan and European corner.

As Barcelona prepared to greet the world as host of the 1992 Olympics, it looked well beyond 1992 and gave itself a thorough face-lift with the "Barcelona 2000" self-improvement program. Barcelonians saw the Olympics as only the beginning.

My biggest frustration in putting this 2- to 22-day plan together was excluding Barcelona. If you're flying into Madrid, it's nearly 400 miles out of your way. By car the trip is not worth it, but by train it's just an easy overnight ride away ($60 each way with a sleeper, 10 hours). If you're coming to Spain from points north, Barcelona is a great and easy first stop. When buying your plane ticket, remember you can go "open jaws" into Barcelona and home from Madrid or Lisbon (or vice versa) for no extra expense.

Barcelona bubbles with life in the narrow alleys of the old Gothic Quarter, along the grand boulevards, and throughout the chic grid-planned new town. While Barcelona had an exciting past as a Roman colony, Visigothic capital, fourteenth-century maritime power, and, in more modern times, a top Mediterranean trading and manufacturing center, it is most enjoyable to throw out the history books and just drift through the city. If you're in the mood to surrender to a city's charms, let it be in Barcelona.

The soul of Barcelona is in its compact core—the Barri Gòtic (Gothic Quarter) and the Ramblas (main boulevard). This is your strolling, shopping, and people-watching nucleus.

Barcelona

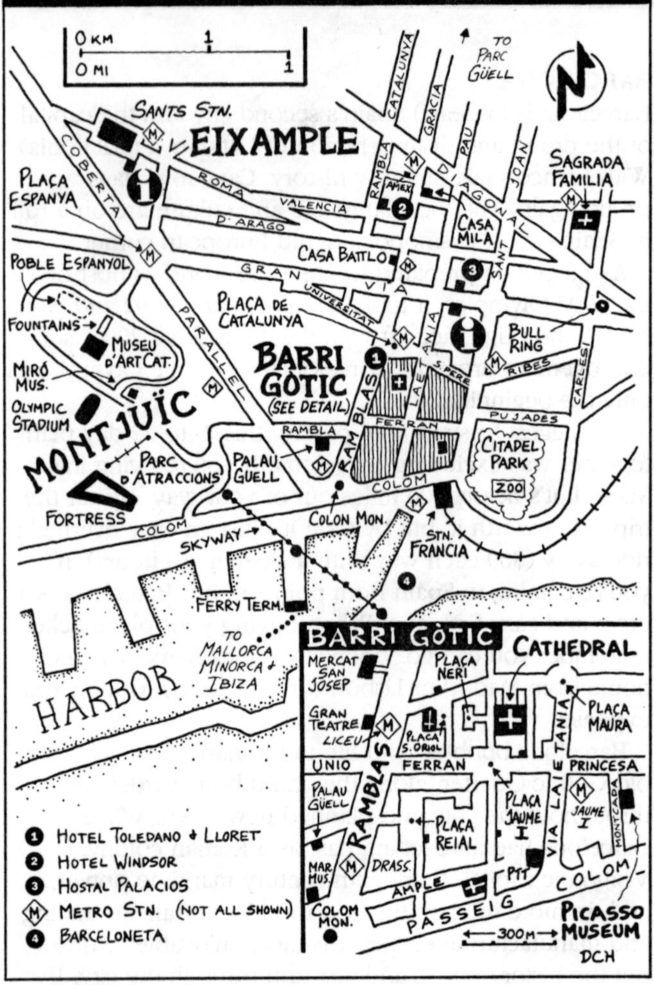

Orientation

The city's sights are widely scattered, but with a basic map and a willingness to figure out the sleek subway system, all is manageable. The subway, which may be Europe's best if not biggest, is often faster than a taxi, dirt-cheap if you buy tickets in strip cards of ten (600 ptas), and connects just about every place you'll visit. Use one of the several helpful tourist offices: if you arrive via the Sants or

Franca train stations, or at the airport, use their very handy information offices. The best Turismo in the city center is at Gran Vía 658 (open Monday-Friday 9:00-19:00, Saturday 9:00-13:30). Another is in the Sants-Central train station (tel. 410-2594). Wherever you go for information, get the large city map, general city information, and brochures listing historic walks, Gaudí sights, Miró sights, and the monthly music and cultural activities. Train information: 322-4142. Telephone code: 93.

The Tourist Bus 100 (Transports Turistics) shuttles tourists on a popular twelve-stop circuit (covering the must-sees, the funicular, and the teleféric for one small ticket) throughout the summer.

Be on guard. Barcelona's thieves thrive on unwary tourists. While the city is generally better-lit and better-policed than ever, more bags and wallets seem to be stolen here than anywhere.

Surprise! Barcelona speaks a different language—Catalán. (Most place-names in this chapter are listed in Catalán.)

Sightseeing Highlights—Barcelona

▲▲▲The Ramblas—More than a "Champs Elysées," this grand Barcelonian axis takes you from rich at the top to rough at the port, a 20-minute walk. You'll find the grand opera house, richly decorated churches, prostitutes, pick-pockets, con men and artists, an outdoor bird market, elegant cafés, great shopping, and people willing to charge more for a shoeshine than you paid for the shoes. When Hans Christian Andersen saw this street over a hundred years ago, he wrote that there could be no doubt that Barcelona was a great city.

"Rambla" means stream in Arabic. It was a drainage ditch along the medieval wall that used to define what is now called the Gothic Quarter. It has five separately named segments but addresses treat it as one mile-long boulevard.

Highlights include (from top to bottom of the Ramblas): **Plaça de Catalunya**, the city's grand central square, transportation hub, and divider of old and new; the old

Mercat de Sant Josep (produce market), an explosion of chicken legs, bags of live snails, stiff fish, delicious oranges, sleeping dogs, and great bars for a cheap breakfast (tortilla española and café con leche); Spain's only real opera house, the luscious **Gran Teatre del Liceu** (200 ptas tours, call 318-9122); the closest thing to Napoleon's cup of tea in town, the elegant neoclassical **Plaça Reial** (royal square), complete with characters who don't need the palm trees to be shady; and the **Palau Güell**, offering the only look at a Gaudí art nouveau interior and, for me, the most enjoyable look at Barcelona's organic architect (metro: Vallarca, open Tuesday-Saturday, 11:00-14:00, 17:00-20:00, 200 ptas). On the Ramblas, you'll find the world's only Chinatown (Barri Xines) with nothing even remotely Chinese in or near it—a dingy, dangerous-after-dark red-light, nightclub district with lots of street girls . . . and a monument to Dr. Fuller, the Canadian who discovered penicillin. At the bottom of the Ramblas stands the Monument a Colom (Columbus Monument) offering an elevator-assisted view from its top (200 ptas, Tuesday-Sunday 9:00-21:00, closed Monday). It is interesting that Barcelona would so honor the man whose discoveries ultimately led to its downfall as a great trading power.

For a look at Barcelona's sea power, before Columbus's discoveries shifted the world's focus west, check out the **Museu Maritim** (Maritime Museum) in the impressive old Drassanes (Royal Shipyards, across the street). It's free and worth a quick look but could be a disappointment, unless you like fleets of seemingly unimportant replicas of old boats all explained in Catalán and Spanish (open Tuesday-Saturday 9:00-13:30, 16:00-19:00, Sunday 10:00-14:00, closed Monday, 200 ptas).

The harbor funicular is a temptation when you see it gliding fitfully across the harbor from a distance. It's expensive (600 ptas) and a time-consuming headache but offers exceptional views of the normally smoggy city. It's open whenever you see the two little red cars dangling (which is usually from 11:00 to 21:00 daily during the summer and off-season weekends); a handy way to get from the attractions of Montjuic to the fine fish restaurants or sandy beaches of Barceloneta.

▲▲▲Barri Gòtic (Gothic Quarter)—Bustling with shops, bars, and night life, the Gothic Quarter is packed with hard-to-be-thrilled-about fourteenth- and fifteenth-century buildings. It's notorious for its seedy night crowd but, except for the part closest to the port, the area now feels safe, thanks to police and countless quaint but very bright streetlights. There is a tangled grab-bag of undiscovered squares, grand squares, schoolyard plazas, art nouveau storefronts, baby flea markets, musty antique shops, classy antique shops, and balconies with jungles behind wrought-iron bars.

The must-see sight is the colossal cathedral, a fine example of Catalán Gothic. Started about 1300, it wasn't completed for 600 years. Like the Gothic churches of Italy, it's not so interested in stretching toward heaven, but is more into massiveness. The heavy *coro* (choir) in the middle confuses the dark and muddled interior. (Why pay to go in from the back when you can see everything for free from the front?) Don't miss the cloister with its wispy garden and worthwhile little museum (cathedral open daily 7:30-13:30, 16:00-19:30).

Shoe-lovers can find the **Museo del Calzado** (two-room shoe museum with the we-try-harder attendant) on Plaça Sant Felip Neri, about a block beyond the outside door of the cloisters (open Tuesday-Sunday, 11:00-14:00, 17:00-20:00, 150 ptas). It stinks so bad, it's fun.

The only other important Barri Gòtic sight is the Palau Reial (royal palace), with museums showing off Barcelona's Roman and medieval history, and the Arxiu de la Corona d'Aragon (Archives of the Kingdom of Aragon) with piles of medieval documents.

▲▲The Picasso Museum—Far and away the best collection of Picasso's (1881-1973) work in Spain, this is a perfect chance to see his earliest sketches and paintings and better understand his genius (metro: Jaume, open Tuesday-Saturday 10:00-20:00, Sunday 10:00-15:00, closed Monday, 500 ptas).

Eixample—Uptown Barcelona is a unique variation on the grid-planned cities you find all over. Barcelona snipped off the building corners to create light and spacious eight-sided squares at every intersection. Wide sidewalks, hardy trees offering shade, chic shops, and plenty of art nouveau (Gaudí and company) fun make the Eixample a refreshing break from the old town. For the best Eixample example, ramble Rambla de Catalunya (unrelated to the more famous Ramblas) and pass through Passeig de Gràcia (metro: Passeig de Gràcia).

▲▲Gaudí's buildings—Barcelona is an architectural scrapbook of the galloping gables and organic curves of hometown boy Antoni Gaudí. Gaudí gave art nouveau a Catalonian twist and they called it "modernisme."

His most famous and persistent work is the unfinished landmark **Sagrada Familia** (Sacred Family) **Church** (metro: Sagrada Familia, open daily 9:00-21:00, 9:00-18:00 off-season, 500 ptas, tel. 455-0247). From 1891 to 1925, Gaudí worked on this monumental church of eight 100-meter spires that will someday dance around a 160-meter granddaddy spire. With the cranes, rusty forests of rebar, and scaffolding requiring a powerful faith, it offers a fun look at a living, growing, bigger-than-life building. Take the lift or the stairs up to the dizzy lookout bridging two spires for a great city view and a gargoyle's-eye perspective of the church. If there's any building on earth I'd like to see, it's the Sagrada Familia . . . finished. Judge for yourself how the controversial current work fits in with the old.

Palau Güell (see above under Ramblas) is a very handy chance to enjoy the only look in town at a Gaudí interior. Curvy.

Two famous Gaudí exteriors laugh down on the crowds that fill Passeig de Gràcia: **Casa Mila** (called La Pedrera, or "the Quarry," at Pg. del Garcia #92, metro: Diagonal, very limited roof-tour tickets given out at 9:45 for 10:00, 11:00, 12:00, and 13:00 tours, tel. 215-3398) with its much photographed roller-coaster of melting ice cream eaves; and **Casa Battlo** (four blocks away at Pg. de Gracia #43, metro: Passeig de Gràcia), its roof a cresting wave of tiles (or is it a dragon's back?). Check out the geometric facade of the house next door by the architect Puig i Cadafalch. This Barcelonian version of keeping up with the Joneses led to the Passeig de Gracia's local nickname "the street of discord." Even if your camera demands it, don't frame your photo from the street—Gaudí died under a streetcar!

For the full dose of Gaudí and a look at the **Gaudí Museum** (metro: Vallarca, open 10:00-14:00, 16:00-19:00, closed Saturdays, 150 ptas), visit his **Parc Güell** (open daily 10:00-21:00, free). To understand it, find a friend with dyslexia and a kaleidoscope (remind yourself that Gaudí's work is a very careful rhythm of color, shapes, and space). For more information on Gaudí, pick up a brochure at the tourist office, or ask one of the many architects who flock to Barcelona to pay homage to their hero. If you're in the mood for more bizarre architecture, check out the **Palau de la Musica** (not by Gaudi, 373 C. Sant Pere Mas Alt). A concert here is memorable.

▲▲▲Montjuïc—The hill overlooking Barcelona's hazy port has always been a show-off. Ages ago it had the impressive fortress. In 1929, it hosted an International Fair, from which most of today's sights originated. And in 1992, the Summer Olympics directed the world's attention to this pincushion of sightseeing attractions. Here's a rundown.

Parc d'Atraccions de Montjuïc (Amusement Park)—This is your best chance to eat, whirl, and hurl with local families (free, daily in summers until late; access from metro: Parallel, by funicular, and the Montjuíc teleférico that stops here on its way up to the fortress).

The **fortress** offers great city views and an impressive military museum (Tuesday-Saturday 10:00-14:00, 16:00-19:00, Sunday 10:00-19:00, 50 ptas).

Fonts Lluminoses (fountains) entertain with music, colored lights, and impressive amounts of water on summer Saturdays and Sundays from 22:00-24:00.

Poble Espanyol (Spanish Village) is a tacky five-acre model village with traditional architecture from all over Spain. This is a cultural education daily, with plenty of shops and craftspeople in action from 9:00 until 19:30,

(600 ptas). After hours it becomes a popular local night spot.

Museu d'Art de Catalunya (Catalonian Art Museum)—Often called "the Prado of Romanesque art," this is a rare and world-class collection of Romanesque frescoes, statues, and paintings, much of it from remote Catalán village churches in the Pyrenees. Also see Gothic work and paintings by the great Spanish masters (open Wednesday-Monday, 9:00-21:00, 500 ptas).

For something a bit more up-to-date, see the **Fundació Joan Miró**, showcasing the modern art talents of yet another Catalonian artist. (Tuesday-Saturday 11:00-19:00, Sunday 10:30-14:30, Thursday until 21:30, closed Monday, 500 ptas).

Sleeping in Barcelona, telephone code: 93, postal codes: see below.

Barcelona is Spain's most expensive city. Still, it has reasonable rooms, so your big decision is which neighborhood. High season is mid-July into October (August is highest), when some prices go up by about 1,000 ptas. Convention season is September and October. Don't be seduced by the classy-appearing lobbies, many of which disguise bad rooms.

Rooms in the Barri Gòtic, postal code: 08002: The Ramblas and Barri Gòtic areas are in the thick of things with plenty of cheap restaurants and bars and more than their share of theft and grime. An abundance of light, policemen, and prosperity seems to be pushing out the pushers and I felt plenty safe so near so much seediness.

Hostal Rey Don Jaume I (pronounced HI-me pre-MEE-ro) is clean, quiet for the area, with bare and basic rooms, all with showers, a block from the city hall and the Jaume I metro stop (inexpensive,C. Jaume I #11, 5 minutes off Ramblas straight down C. de Ferran, tel. 315-4161).

Hotel Jardi is a hardworking, plain, and clean place located on the happiest little square in the Gothic Quarter (inexpensive, a block off the Ramblas on Plaça Sant Josep Oriol #1, tel. 301-5900, fax 318 3664).

Hotel Roma is ideally located right on the elegant-but-ramshackle Plaça Reial, 50 yards off the Ramblas. It offers basic, bare rooms, all with showers, some with fine balconies overlooking the moonlit square (inexpensive, Plaça Reial #11, 08002 Barcelona, tel. 302-0366 and 302-0416, fax 301 1839). The Hotel Roma people also run the similar **Hotel Comércio** nearby.

Hotels at the top (decent and comfortable) end of the Ramblas, postal code: 08010. Hotel Toledano's elevator takes you high above the noise and into the *zona bella vista*; request a view balcony. It's small and folksy and English is spoken (inexpensive, Rambla de Canaletas 138, tel. 301-0872, fax 412 3142). The nearby **Hotel Lloret** is a good value right on the Ramblas, English spoken (moderate, Rambla Canaletas 125, tel. 317-3366, fax 301 9283).

Huéspedes Santa Ana, nearby on a small pedestrain street that crosses the Ramblas, has plain, clean, nothing-special rooms, no English spoken (cheap, C. Santa Ana 23, tel. 301-2246). A bit further away, the **Hostal Palacios** is a grand little place on Gran Vía across from the tourist info (inexpensive, Gran Vía Cortes Catalanas #629, tel. 301-3792).

Hotels in Eixample, postal code: 08008: For a more elegant and boulevardian neighborhood, sleep in Eixample, 5 minutes by subway from the action. **Hostal Residencia Windsor** was the only budget place I found that my piano teacher could enjoy. Great locale, classy, spotlessly clean, friendly (inexpensive, one floor up, Rambla Cataluña 84, tel. 215-1198). **Pensión Fani** is a rare budget find for women only (as Aussies already may have guessed). Clean and quiet, with no one speaking English or watching soccer on TV (1000 ptas per person in one- or two-bed rooms, Valencia 278, 2nd floor, tel. 215-3645 and 215-3044).

Youth Hostels: Hostal de Joves (900 ptas per person, Pg. de Pujades 29, next to Parc de la Ciutadella and metro: Marina, tel. 300-3104, open 7:00-10:00 and 15:00-00:00) is clean and well-run. The **Hostal Verge de Montserrat** (1000-1300 ptas per person, Pg. Mare de Deu del Coll 41, near Parc Güell, bus #28 from Pl. Catalunya near Parc Güell or metro: Lesseps, tel. 210 5151) is open all day and much cheerier and worth the extra commute time. **Hostal Pere Tarres** (C. Numancia 149, near the Sants-Central station and metro: Les Corts, tel. 410-2309) is also good and accepts nonmembers willing to pay a bit more for not joining the club.

Eating in Barcelona

Barcelona, the capital of Catalonian cuisine, offers a tremendous variety of colorful places to eat. The harbor area, especially Barceloneta, is famous for fish. The best tapa bars are in the Barri Gòtic and around the Picasso Museum. **Los Caracoles** at Escudelleros 14 is a sort of Spanish Hofbräuhaus—huge and always packed. My favorite place for local-style food in a local-style setting is **Restaurant Agut** (Calle Gignas 16, tel. 315-1709, huge servings, inexpensive, closed in July). **El Portalon** at C Banos Nuevos 20 in the bowels of the Gothic Quarter drips with atmosphere and offers good food and drink. **Restaurante Bidasoa** (near the waterfront in the Gothic Quarter (C. En Serra #21, tel. 318-1063) is also characteristic and inexpensive. For fewer tourists, less color, and more class, you can find good reasonable meals in the Gràcia and Eixample districts.

IBERIAN HISTORY

The cultural landscape of present-day Spain and Portugal was shaped by the various civilizations that settled on the peninsula. Iberia's warm and sunny weather and fertile soil attracted all early Mediterranean peoples.

The Greeks came to Cádiz around 1100 B.C., followed by the Romans, who occupied the country for almost 1,000 years until A.D. 400. The Roman influence remained long after the empire crumbled, including cultural values, materials, and building techniques, even Roman-style farming equipment, which was used well into the nineteenth century. And, of course, wine.

Moors (711–1492)
The Moors—North Africans of the Moslem faith who occupied Spain—had the greatest cultural influence on Spanish and Portuguese history. They arrived on the Rock of Gibraltar in A.D. 711 and moved north. In the incredibly short time of seven years, the Moors completely conquered the peninsula.

They established their power and Moslem culture—but in a subtle way. Non-Moslems were tolerated and often rose to positions of wealth and power; Jewish culture flourished. Instead of blindly suppressing the natives by force, the Moors used their superior power and knowledge to develop whatever they found. For example, they encouraged the making of wine, although for religious reasons they themselves weren't allowed to drink alcohol.

The Moors ruled for more than 700 years (711–1492). Throughout that time, pockets of Christianity remained. Local Christian kings fought against the Moors whenever they could, whittling away at the Moslem empire, gaining more and more land. The last Moorish stronghold, Granada, fell to the Christians in 1492.

The slow, piecemeal process of the Reconquista (Reconquest) split the peninsula into the two independent states of Portugal and Spain. In 1139, Alfonso Henriques conquered the Moors near present-day Beja in southern

Portugal and proclaimed himself king of the area. By 1200, the Christian state of Portugal already had the borders it does today, making it the oldest unchanged state in Europe. The rest of the peninsula was a loosely knit collection of smaller kingdoms until 1469, when Fernando II of Aragon married Isabel of Castilla. Known as the "Catholic Monarchs," they united the other kingdoms under their rule.

The Golden Age (1500–1700)

The expulsion of the Moors set the stage for the rise of Portugal and Spain as naval powers and colonial superpowers—the Golden Age. The Spaniards, fueled by the religious fervor of their Reconquista of the Moslems, were interested in spreading Christianity to the newly discovered New World. Wherever they landed, they tried to Christianize the natives—with the sword, if necessary.

The Portuguese expansion was motivated more by economic concerns. Their excursions overseas were planned, cool, and rational. They colonized the nearby coasts of Africa first, progressing slowly to Asia and South America.

Through exploration (and exploitation) of the colonies, tremendous amounts of gold came into each country. Art and courtly life developed fast in this Golden Age. The aristocracy and the clergy were swimming in money.

The French baroque architecture that you'll see (such as La Granja and the Royal Palace in Madrid) is a reminder that Spain was ruled by the French Bourbon family in the eighteenth century.

Slow Decline

The fast money from the colonies kept Spain and Portugal from seeing the dangers at home. Great Britain and the Netherlands also were becoming naval powers, defeating the Spanish Armada in 1588. The Portuguese imported everything, didn't grow their own wheat any more, and neglected their fields.

During the centuries when science and technology in all other European countries developed as never before, Spain and Portugal were occupied with their failed colonial politics. Endless battles, wars of succession, revolutions, and counter-revolutions weakened the countries. In this chaos, there was no chance to develop democratic forms of life. Dictators in both countries made the rich richer and kept the masses underprivileged.

During World Wars I and II, both countries stayed neutral, uninterested in foreign policy as long as there was quiet in their own states. In the 1930s, Spain suffered a bloody and bitter Civil War between fascist and democratic forces. The fascist dictator Franco prevailed, ruling the country until his death in the 1970s.

Democracy in Spain and Portugal is still young. After an unbloody revolution, Portugal held democratic elections in 1975. After 41 years of dictatorship, Spain had elections in 1977.

Today, socialists are in power in both countries. They've adopted a policy of balance to save the young democracies and fight problems such as unemployment and foreign debts—with moderate success. Spain recently joined the European Economic Community.

ART AND ARCHITECTURE

ART

The "Big Three" in Spanish painting are El Greco, Velázquez, and Goya.

El Greco (1541–1614) exemplifies the spiritual fervor of so much Spanish art. The drama, the surreal colors, and the intentionally unnatural distortion have the intensity of a religious vision.

Diego Velázquez (1599–1660) went to the opposite extreme. His masterful court portraits are studies in realism and cool detachment from his subjects.

Goya (1746–1828) matched Velázquez's technique but not his detachment. He let his liberal tendencies shine through in unflattering portraits of royalty and in emotional scenes of abuse of power. He unleashed his inner passions in the eerie, nightmarish canvases of his last, "dark," stage.

Not quite in the "Big Three," the Spanish artist, Murillo (1618–1682), painted a dreamy world of religious visions. His pastel, soft-focus works of cute baby Jesuses and pure radiant Virgin Marys helped make Catholic doctrine palatable to the common folk at a time when many were defecting to Protestantism.

You'll also find plenty of foreign art in Spain's museums. Spain had piles of wealthy aristocrats during its Golden Age. And they bought wagonloads of the most popular art of the time—Italian Renaissance and baroque works by Titian and Tintoretto, and so on. They also loaded up on paintings by Rubens, Bosch, and Brueghel from the Low Countries, which were under Spanish rule.

In this century, Pablo Picasso (don't miss his mural, *Guernica*), Joan Miró, and surrealist Salvador Dali have made their marks. Fans wishing to say "Hello, Dali" should check out his museum in the town of Figueres north of Barcelona.

ARCHITECTURE

The two most fertile periods of architectural innovation in Spain and Portugal were during the Moorish occupation and in the Golden Age. Otherwise, Spanish architecture follows many of the same trends as the rest of Europe.

The Moors brought Middle-Eastern styles with them, such as the horseshoe arch, minarets, and floor plans designed for mosques. Islam forbids the sculpting or painting of human or animal figures ("graven images"), so artists expressed their creativity with elaborate geometric patterns. The ornate stucco of the Alhambra, the striped arches of Córdoba's mosque, and decorative colored tiles are evidence of the Moorish sense of beauty. Mozarabic and Mudejar styles blended Islamic and Christian elements.

As the Christians slowly reconquered the country, they turned their fervor into stone, building churches in both the heavy, fortress-of-God Romanesque style (Santiago de Compostela) and in the lighter, heaven-reaching, stained-glass Gothic style (Barcelona, Toledo, Sevilla). Gothic was an import from France, trickling into conservative Spain long after it swept through Europe.

The money reaped and raped from Spain's colonies in the Golden Age (1500–1650) spurred new construction. Churches and palaces were built using the solid, geometric style of the Italian Renaissance (El Escorial) and the more ornamented baroque. Ornamentation reached unprecedented heights in Spain, culminating in the Plateresque style of stonework, so called because it resembles intricate silver filigree work. In Portugal, the highly ornamented style is called Manueline. The Belem Tower in Lisbon is its best example.

After the Golden Age, innovation in both countries died out, and most buildings from the eighteenth and nineteenth centuries follow predictable European trends.

Spain's major contribution to modern architecture is the art nouveau work of Antoni Gaudí early in this century. Most of his "cake-left-out-in-the-rain" buildings, with their asymmetrical designs and sinuous lines, can be found in Barcelona.

History and Art Terms

Alcazaba	Moorish castle.
Alcázar	Initially a Moorish fortified castle, later a residence.
Ayuntamiento	Town hall.
Azulejo	Blue or colored tiles.
Feria	Fair.
Inquisition	Religious and civil courts begun in the Middle Ages for trying heretics and sinners. Punishment ranged from prayer to imprisonment, torture, and death. An estimated 2,000 heretics were burned at the stake during the reign of one notorious Grand Inquisitor.
Moros	Moors. Moslems from North Africa.
Moriscos	Moors converted to Christianity after the victory of the Catholics.
Mozarabs	Christians under Moorish rule.

BULLFIGHTING

The Spanish bullfight is as much a ritual as it is a sport. While no two bullfights are the same, they unfold along a strict pattern.

The ceremony begins punctually with a parade of participants around the ring. Then the trumpet sounds, the "Gate of Fear" opens, and the leading player—*el toro*—thunders in. An angry half-ton animal is an awesome sight even from the cheap seats.

The fight is divided into three acts. Act I is designed to size up the bull and wear him down. The matador (from the word *matar*—to kill), with help from his assistants, attracts the bull with the shake of the cape, then directs the bull past his body, as close as his bravery allows. After a few passes, the *picadors* enter, mounted on horseback, to spear the powerful swollen lump of muscle at the back of the bull's neck. This lowers the bull's head and weakens the thrust of his horns.

In Act II, the matador's assistants (*banderilleros*) continue to enrage and weaken the bull. The unarmed banderillero charges the charging bull and, leaping acrobatically across the bull's path, plunges brightly colored, barbed sticks into the bull's vital neck muscle.

After a short intermission during which the matador may, according to tradition, ask permission to kill the bull and dedicate the kill to someone in the crowd, the final, lethal Act III begins.

The matador tries to dominate and tire the bull with hypnotic capework. A good pass is when the matador stands completely still while the bull charges past. Then the matador thrusts a sword between the animal's shoulderblades for the kill. A quick kill is not always easy, and the matador may have to make several bloody thrusts before the sword stays in.

Throughout the fight, the crowd shows its approval or impatience. Shouts of "Olé!" or "Torero!" mean they like what they see—whistling or rhythmic hand-clapping greets cowardice and incompetence.

After an exceptional fight, the crowd may wave white handkerchiefs to ask that the matador be awarded the bull's ear or tail. A brave bull, though dead, gets a victory lap from the mule team on his way to the slaughterhouse. Then the trumpet sounds, and a new bull barges in to face a fresh matador. A typical bullfight lasts about 3 hours and consists of six separate fights—three matadors fighting two bulls each.

For a closer look at bullfighting by an American aficionado, read Hemingway's classic *Death in the Afternoon.*

HOURS, SIESTAS, AND FIESTAS

Iberia is a land of strange and frustrating schedules. Most businesses respect the afternoon siesta. When it is 100° in the shade and you're wandering dusty, deserted streets looking for a bank to change money, you'll understand why.

Generally, shops are open 9:00 to 13:00 and 15:00 or 16:00 to 19:00 or 20:00, longer in touristy places. On Saturdays, shops are often open only in the morning, all are closed Sundays. Banks are open Monday-Friday from 9:00 to 14:00 (or 13:00, or 13:30), Saturdays from 9:00 to 13:00 and, very occasionally, Monday-Friday 15:30 to 16:30. Restaurants open very late. Museums are generally open from 10:00 to 13:00 and from 15:00 to 19:00, though the important ones stay open at siesta. The times listed in this book are for the tourist season. In winter, most museums and sights close an hour early.

There are many regional and surprise holidays. Regular nationwide holidays are:

Portugal—January 1, April 25, May 1, June 10 (national holiday), August 15, October 5, November 1, December 1, December 8, and December 25.

Spain—January 1, January 6, March 19, May 1, June 24, June 29, July 18, July 25, August 15, October 12, November 1, December 8, December 25, Good Friday and Easter, Corpus Christi (early June).

Spain and Portugal erupt with fiestas and celebrations throughout the year. For a complete listing, in English, of upcoming festivals, call or write to the Spanish or Portuguese National Tourist Office (see below).

BASIC INFORMATION

Money

The *peseta* (pta) is the basic monetary unit of Spain. One peseta is worth slightly less than a U.S. penny. In the summer of '93, there were 130 ptas in $1US. One hundred pesetas = about 75 cents. So a 200 pta *helado* (ice cream) costs about $1.50 and a 3000 pta room is $23. Spanish coins come in 1, 5 10, 25, 100 and 500 pta amounts, while bills come in 1000, 2000, 5000, and 10000 denominations.

The Portuguese *escudo* (somewhat confusingly indicated by a $ placed after the number) is worth slightly less—in the summer of '93 there were 160 escudos in $1US. One hundred escudos = about 65 cents. To convert escudos to dollars cover the two numbers to the left of the $ sign. Two-thirds of the remaining amount = amount in dollars. So a meal costing 2100$ escudos is about $14. Portuguese coins come in 1, 2 1/2, 5, 10, 20, 50, 100, and 200 amounts, while bills come in 500, 1000, 2000, 5000, and 10000 denominations.

National Tourist Offices

Some of the best information for planning your trip is just a postcard away. The National Tourist Office of each country is more than happy to send brochures and information on all aspects of travel in their country. The more specific your request (e.g., pousadas, castles, hiking), the better they can help you.

National Tourist Office of Spain: 665 Fifth Ave., New York, NY 10022 (tel. 212/759-8822); 845 N. Michigan Ave., Chicago, IL 60611 (tel. 312/642-1992); and 8383 Wilshire Blvd. #960, Beverly Hills, CA 90211 (tel. 213/658-7188). In Canada: 102 Bloor St. W., Toronto, Ontario M5S 1MB (tel. 416/961-4079).

Portuguese National Tourist Office: 590 Fifth Ave., New York, NY 10036 (tel. 212/354-4403); 60 Bloor St. W., #1005, Toronto, Ontario, Canada M4W 3B8 (tel. 416/921-4925).

Moroccan National Tourist Office: 20 East 46th St., New York, NY 10017 (tel. 212/557-2520); 2001 rue Université #1460, Montreal, Quebec, Canada PQH3A 2A6 (tel. 514/842-8111).

Telephone Tips

Using the telephone in your travels in Iberia is a bit more complicated but just as important as elsewhere in Europe. A few tips will minimize frustration:

Country codes (calling to): Spain 34, Portugal 351, Morocco 212

U.S. to Spain: 011/34/area code (without the long distance prefix 9)/number

U.S. to Portugal: 011/351/area code (without the long distance prefix 0)/number

Spain or Portugal to U.S.: 07/1/area code/number

Spain to Portugal: 07/351/area code/number

Portugal to Spain: 00/34/area code/number

Long distance in Spain: 9/area code/number

Long distance in Portugal: 0/area code/number

Directory assistance in Spain: 003; in Portugal: 13

AT&T operator: 900 99 00 11 in Spain and 05 017 1288 in Portugal

MCI operator: 900 99 00 14 in Spain and 05 017 1234 in Portugal.

SPRINT operator: 900 99 00 13 in Spain and 05 017 1877 in Portugal.

That is straightforward enough. But confusion is caused by the fact that numbers vary from 3 to 7 digits and in either country some numbers are listed with area codes while others aren't. Also some numbers are listed with the long distance prefix (9 in Spain and 0 in Portugal). If you can't get through, analyze the problem from the number-of-digits point of view and try again with more or less digits. Coin-operated phones are rapidly being replaced by card-operated phones, making long distance calling a breeze. Cards are normally purchased at the post office, tourist offices and *tabaco* shops—buy one upon entering the country. To use the card, simply insert your card in the slot on the phone, wait for a dial tone and digital readout to show how much value remains on your card and dial away—the cost of the call is automatically deducted from your card. The telephone is the best iron for wrinkled travels.

Calls to the U.S. are very expensive, as are calls from your hotel, but calling home becomes almost painless when you have and use an AT&T or MCI credit card. Just dial their magic toll-free number (see above) and an American operator will put you through, billing your card their $2.50 service fee plus the (much cheaper per minute) American long distance rate.

Telephone Area Codes

Spain 34 (country code)
Madrid 1
Segovia 11
Salamanca 23
Ciudad Rodrigo 23
Sevilla 54
Ronda 52
Málaga 52
Granada 58
Toledo 25
Barcelona 3
Santiago 81
(To dial long-distance numbers within Spain, precede each area code with 9.)

Portugal 351 (country code)
Lisbon 1
Nazaré 62
Obidos 62
Évora 66
Coimbra 39
Lagos and Salema 82
Tavira 81

CLIMATE

1st line, avg. daily low; 2nd line, avg. daily high; 3rd line, days of no rain

	J	F	M	A	M	J	J	A	S	O	N	D
PORTUGAL	47	57	50	52	56	60	64	65	62	58	52	48
Lagos/Algarve	61	61	63	67	73	77	83	84	80	73	66	62
	22	19	20	24	27	29	31	31	28	26	22	22
	46	47	49	52	56	60	63	64	62	57	52	47
Lisbon	56	58	61	64	69	75	79	80	76	69	62	57
	22	20	21	23	25	28	30	30	26	24	20	21
SPAIN	33	35	40	44	50	57	62	62	56	48	40	35
Madrid	47	51	47	64	71	80	87	86	77	66	54	48
	22	19	20	21	22	24	28	29	24	23	20	22
	42	44	47	51	57	63	69	69	65	58	50	44
Barcelona	56	57	61	64	71	77	81	82	67	61	62	57
	26	21	24	22	23	25	27	26	23	23	23	25
	47	48	51	55	60	66	70	72	68	61	53	48
Malaga	61	62	64	69	74	80	84	85	81	74	67	62
	25	22	23	25	28	29	31	30	28	27	22	25

INDEX

Rick Steves'

EUROPE THROUGH THE BACK DOOR CATALOG

All items are field tested, discount priced (prices include tax and shipping), completely guaranteed, and highly recommended for European travel.

CONVERTIBLE BACK DOOR BAG $75

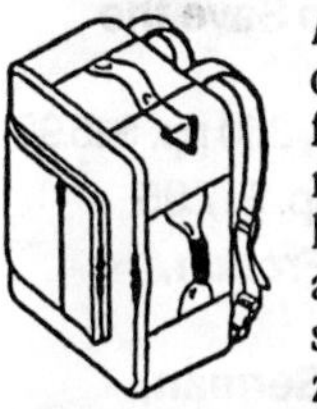

At 9"x21"x13" our specially designed, sturdy bag is maximum carry-on-the-plane size (fits under the seat) and your key to footloose and fancy-free travel. Made of rugged water resistant cordura nylon, it converts easily from a smart looking suitcase to a handy rucksack. It has padded hide-away shoulder straps, top and side handles, and a detachable shoulder strap (for use as a suitcase). Lockable perimeter zippers allow easy access to the roomy 2,500 cubic inch central compartment. Two large outside compartments are perfect for frequently used items. A nylon stuff bag is also included. Rick Steves and over 40,000 other Back Door travelers have lived out of these bags all around the world. Available in black, grey, navy blue and teal green.

MONEYBELT $8

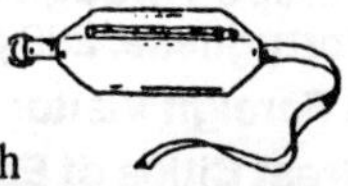

Absolutely required for European travel, our sturdy nylon, ultra-light, under-the-pants pouch is just big enough to carry your essentials (passport, airline tickets, travelers checks, and so on) comfortably. Rick won't travel without one, and neither should you. Comes in neutral beige, with a nylon zipper. One size fits all.

EUROPEAN RAILPASSES

We sell the full range of European railpasses, and with every Eurailpass we give you these important extras -- ***free:*** Rick Steves' 90-minute "How to get the most out of your railpass" video; your choice of one of Rick's seven "2 to 22 Days in..." guidebooks; and our comments on your 1-page proposed itinerary. Call us for a free copy of our 48-page ***1994 Back Door Guide to European Railpasses.***

BACK DOOR 'BEST OF EUROPE' TOURS

We offer a variety of European tours for those who want to travel in the Back Door style, but without the transportation and hotel hassles. These tours feature small groups, our own guides, Back Door accomodations, and lots of physical exercise. Our tours aren't for everyone, but they may be just the ticket for you. Call us for details.

FREE TRAVEL NEWSLETTER/CATALOG

Give us a call at (206) 771-8303, and we'll send you our free newsletter / catalog packed full of info on budget travel, books, maps, videos railpasses and tours. We'll help you travel better ***because*** you're on a budget -- not in spite of it.

Prices are good through 1994 (maybe longer), and include tax and shipping (allow 2 to 3 weeks). Sorry, no credit cards or phone orders. Send checks in US $ to:

Europe Through the Back Door ❖ 109 Fourth Avenue North
PO Box 2009, Edmonds, WA 98020 ❖ Phone: (206)771-8303

Other Books from John Muir Publications

Asia Through the Back Door, 4th ed., 400 pp. $16.95 (available 7/93)

Belize: A Natural Destination, 336 pp. $16.95

Costa Rica: A Natural Destination, 2nd ed., 310 pp. $16.95

Elderhostels: The Students' Choice, 2nd ed., 304 pp. $15.95

Environmental Vacations: Volunteer Projects to Save the Planet, 2nd ed., 248 pp. $16.95

Europe 101: History & Art for the Traveler, 4th ed., 350 pp. $15.95

Europe Through the Back Door, 11th ed., 432 pp. $17.95

Europe Through the Back Door Phrase Book: French, 160 pp. $4.95

Europe Through the Back Door Phrase Book: German, 160 pp. $4.95

Europe Through the Back Door Phrase Book: Italian, 168 pp. $4.95

Europe Through the Back Door Phrase Book: Spanish & Portuguese, 288 pp. $4.95

A Foreign Visitor's Guide to America, 224 pp. $12.95

Great Cities of Eastern Europe, 256 pp. $16.95

Guatemala: A Natural Destination, 336 pp. $16.95

Indian America: A Traveler's Companion, 4th ed., 448 pp. $17.95 (available 7/93)

Interior Furnishings Southwest, 256 pp. $19.95

Mona Winks: Self-Guided Tours of Europe's Top Museums, 2nd ed., 448 pp. $16.95

Opera! The Guide to Western Europe's Great Houses, 296 pp. $18.95

Paintbrushes and Pistols: How the Taos Artists Sold the West, 288 pp. $17.95

The People's Guide to Mexico, 9th ed., 608 pp. $18.95

Ranch Vacations: The Complete Guide to Guest and Resort, Fly-Fishing, and Cross-Country Skiing Ranches, 2nd ed., 396 pp. $18.95

The Shopper's Guide to Art and Crafts in the Hawaiian Islands, 272 pp. $13.95

The Shopper's Guide to Mexico, 224 pp. $9.95

Understanding Europeans, 272 pp. $14.95

Undiscovered Islands of the Caribbean, 3rd ed., 288 pp. $14.95

Undiscovered Islands of the Mediterranean, 2nd ed., 224 pp. $13.95

Undiscovered Islands of the U.S. and Canadian West Coast, 288 pp. $12.95

Unique Colorado, 112 pp. $10.95 (available 6/93)
Unique Florida, 112 pp. $10.95 (available 7/93)
Unique New Mexico, 112 pp. $10.95 (available 6/93)
A Viewer's Guide to Art: A Glossary of Gods, People, and Creatures, 144 pp. $10.95
The Visitor's Guide to the Birds of the Eastern National Parks: United States and Canada, 410 pp. $15.95

2 to 22 Days Series
Each title offers 22 flexible daily itineraries useful for planning vacations of any length. Aside from valuable general information, included are "must see" attractions *and* hidden "jewels."
2 to 22 Days in the American Southwest, 1993 ed., 176 pp. $10.95
2 to 22 Days in Asia, 1993 ed., 176 pp. $9.95
2 to 22 Days in Australia, 1993 ed., 192 pp. $9.95
2 to 22 Days in California, 1993 ed., 192 pp. $9.95
2 to 22 Days in Europe, 1993 ed., 288 pp. $13.95
2 to 22 Days in Florida, 1993 ed., 192 pp. $10.95
2 to 22 Days in France, 1993 ed., 192 pp. $10.95
2 to 22 Days in Germany, Austria, & Switzerland, 1993 ed., 224 pp. $10.95
2 to 22 Days in Great Britain, 1993 ed., 192 pp. $10.95
2 to 22 Days Around the Great Lakes, 1993 ed., 192 pp. $10.95
2 to 22 Days in Hawaii, 1993 ed., 192 pp. $9.95
2 to 22 Days in Italy, 208 pp. $10.95
2 to 22 Days in New England, 1993 ed., 192 pp. $10.95
2 to 22 Days in New Zealand, 1993 ed., 192 pp. $9.95
2 to 22 Days in Norway, Sweden, & Denmark, 1993 ed., 192 pp. $10.95
2 to 22 Days in the Pacific Northwest, 1993 ed., 192 pp. $10.95
2 to 22 Days in the Rockies, 1993 ed., 192 pp. $10.95
2 to 22 Days in Spain & Portugal, 192 pp. $10.95
2 to 22 Days in Texas, 1993 ed., 192 pp. $9.95
2 to 22 Days in Thailand, 1993 ed., 180 pp. $9.95
22 Days (or More) Around the World, 1993 ed., 264 pp. $12.95

Automotive Titles
How to Keep Your VW Alive, 15th ed., 464 pp. $21.95
How to Keep Your Subaru Alive 480 pp. $21.95
How to Keep Your Toyota Pickup Alive 392 pp. $21.95
How to Keep Your Datsun/Nissan Alive 544 pp. $21.95
The Greaseless Guide to Car Care Confidence, 224 pp. $14.95
Off-Road Emergency Repair & Survival, 160 pp. $9.95

TITLES FOR YOUNG READERS AGES 8 AND UP

"Kidding Around" Travel Guides for Young Readers
All the "Kidding Around" Travel guides are 64 pages and $9.95 paper, except for **Kidding Around Spain** and **Kidding Around the National Parks of the Southwest**, which are 108 pages and $12.95 paper.

Kidding Around Atlanta
Kidding Around Boston,2nd ed.
Kidding Around Chicago, 2nd ed.
Kidding Around the Hawaiian Islands
Kidding Around London
Kidding Around Los Angeles
Kidding Around the National Parks of the Southwest
Kidding Around New York City, 2nd ed.
Kidding Around Paris
Kidding Around Philadelphia
Kidding Around San Diego
Kidding Around San Francisco
Kidding Around Santa Fe
Kidding Around Seattle
Kidding Around Spain
Kidding Around Washington, D.C., 2nd ed.

"Extremely Weird" Series for Young Readers. Written by Sarah Lovett, each is 48 pages and $9.95 paper.
Extremely Weird Bats
Extremely Weird Birds
Extremely Weird Endangered Species
Extremely Weird Fishes
Extremely Weird Frogs
Extremely Weird Insects
Extremely Weird Mammals (available 8/93)
Extremely Weird Micro Monsters (available 8/93)
Extremely Weird Primates
Extremely Weird Reptiles
Extremely Weird Sea Creatures
Extremely Weird Snakes (available 8/93)
Extremely Weird Spiders

"Masters of Motion" Series for Young Readers. Each title is 48 pages and $9.95 paper.
How to Drive an Indy Race Car
How to Fly a 747
How to Fly the Space Shuttle

"X-ray Vision" Series for Young Readers. Each title is 48 pages and $9.95 paper.
Looking Inside Cartoon Animation
Looking Inside Sports Aerodynamics

Looking Inside the Brain
Looking Inside Sunken Treasure
Looking Inside Telescopes and the Night Sky

Multicultural Titles for Young Readers
Native Artists of North America, 48 pp. $14.95 hardcover
The Indian Way: Learning to Communicate with Mother Earth, 114 pp. $9.95
The Kids' Environment Book: What's Awry and Why, 192 pp. $13.95
Kids Explore America's African-American Heritage, 112 pp. $8.95
Kids Explore America's Hispanic Heritage, 112 pp. $7.95

Environmental Titles for Young Readers
Rads, Ergs, and Cheeseburgers: The Kids' Guide to Energy and the Environment, 108 pp. $12.95
Habitats: Where the Wild Things Live, 48 pp. $9.95
The Kids' Environment Book: What's Awry and Why, 192 pp. $13.95

Ordering Information
Please check your local bookstore for our books, or call 1-800-888-7504 to order direct from us. All orders are shipped via UPS; see chart below to calculate your shipping charge to U.S. destinations. **No P.O. Boxes please; we must have a street address to ensure delivery.** If the book you request is not available, we will hold your check until we can ship it. Foreign orders will be shipped surface rate unless otherwise requested; please enclose $3.00 for the first item and $1.00 for each additional item.

For U.S. Orders Totaling	Add
Up to $15.00	$4.25
$15.01 to $45.00	$5.25
$45.01 to $75.00	$6.25
$75.01 or more	$7.25

Methods of Payment
Check, money order, American Express, MasterCard, or Visa. We cannot be responsible for cash sent through the mail. For credit card orders, include your card number, expiration date, and your signature, or call (800) 888-7504. American Express card orders can be shipped only to billing address of cardholder. Sorry, no C.O.D.'s. Residents of sunny New Mexico, add 6.125% tax to total.

Address all orders and inquiries to:
John Muir Publications
P.O. Box 613
Santa Fe, NM 87504
(505) 982-4078
(800) 888-7504